lessons
for the worship team

a resource for pastors and worship leaders

Dave Patterson
and Joseph Zwanziger

abc Book Publishing

leader's manual

Published by

ABC Book Publishing

AbcBookPublishing.com
Printed in U.S.A.

Lessons for the Worship Team
A resource for Pastors and Worship Leaders

10 Digit ISBN: 1-60185-031-X
13 Digit ISBN (EAN): 978-1-60185-031-7

About the Authors

Dave Patterson

Dave Patterson and his wife Donna are the Senior/Founding Pastors of The Father's House. Dave also serves on the Apostolic Leadership Team of Ministers Fellowship International. Dave and Donna moved to Vacaville in the summer of 1996 and launched the church in March of 1997. They have been married and involved in worship ministry and church leadership for over 25 years.

Dave also authored the book, *Equipping the Worship Team: Principles of Excellence and Practical Tools for Worship Leaders.*

Joseph Zwanziger

Joseph Zwanziger is the Worship Pastor and Director of the School of Worship Arts at The Father's House and has been leading worship for over ten years. Joseph is one of the main songwriters at The Father's House and has produced several of the worship albums of the church. He and his wife Tosha pastor the various aspects of the worship ministry at The Father's House together.

Table of Contents

Introduction
  How We Got It 9
  How to Use It 11
Chapter 1 - Being a Gift 13
Chapter 2 - Coming Into His Presence Pt. 1 – Thanksgiving 19
Chapter 3 - Coming Into His Presence Pt. 2 – Praise 23
Chapter 4 - Countenance 27
Chapter 5 - Creating a Culture of Joy 33
Chapter 6 - Creating a Prophetic Atmosphere 39
Chapter 7 - Excellence 45
Chapter 8 - Musical Preparation 51
Chapter 9 - Platform Protocol 57
Chapter 10 - Plowing in Worship 63
Chapter 11 - Production Elements in Worship 69
Chapter 12 - Rehearsal Protocol 75
Chapter 13 - Spiritual Unity in the Worship Team – Pt. 1 73
Chapter 14 - Spiritual Unity in the Worship Team – Pt. 2 85
Chapter 15 - Stewardship of Our Gifts 89
Chapter 16 - The Anointing 95
Chapter 17 - The Language of Worship 101
Chapter 18 - The Personal Priorities of a Worship Minister 107
Chapter 19 - The Priorities of Worship Ministry 113
Chapter 20 - The Snare of Comparison 119
Chapter 21 - Where God Lives 125
Chapter 22 - Worship in Spirit 131
Chapter 23 - Worship in Truth 137
Chapter 24 - Worship Mentors & Models 143
Appendix 151

Introduction

How We Got It

Since the beginning, The Father's House has been built on a passion for worship and the presence of God. I guess you could call us "presence junkies." Ever since the inception of the church, God has blessed us with musicians and singers who share this same passion for worship. However, any person who has been in leadership for any length of time knows that good-intentioned people are never enough to sustain a ministry for the long-haul.

So, the worship ministry here at The Father's House has been built on times in the presence of God together as a team as well as times of intentional teaching on worship and worship ministry. It has been a priority for us to make sure that we not only have a collection of worship ministers who have a command of their "craft" but also an accurate Biblical foundation for why they do what they do.

Over the years, we've been delivering teachings on worship to our teams in different ways, but the goal and heart has always been the same: We want every member of our worship ministry to understand why we do what we do and how we do it. As our church and worship ministry have grown and evolved over the years, so too have our leadership methods.

When our church reached about 10 years old, we experienced a healthy, natural amount of turnover that is associated with people being "launched" from The Father's House to help in church plants, resourcing other churches in our network, and so forth. So, we intentionally focused on reproducing our team here even more. God was faithful and brought the musicians when we needed them, but we had to intentionally focus on making sure that this new "crop" of musicians were grounded in the same DNA that caused our church to be what it is.

This collection of lessons for the worship team is the result of my efforts to infuse that DNA into every person in our worship ministry. My heart (Joseph writing) was to make it easy for every worship leader in our worship ministry to be able to bring relevant and impactful teachings to our worship rehearsal without having to spend the hours and hours it takes to develop them. It didn't take long to realize, "Hey, I bet that worship leaders and pastors from all kinds of local churches would benefit from these lessons as well."

So here it is. Our heart behind these lessons is that your worship ministry would be strong, vibrant, and a powerhouse of skill, excellence, and knowledge as each member steps up to minister, week in and week out. We've seen how powerful it is to put the knowledge of the Word in the hearts of our teams, and we want to empower you to do the same for your team. We know how hard it is to talk about the "real" issues of worship ministry, and so we hope these lessons help to facilitate that discussion a little better.

Our prayer is that your worship ministry would experience the blessings we have experienced through these lessons over the years. We pray that you, as the leader, would be strengthened, refreshed, and revitalized as you carry the torch and lead the way. And most of all, we pray that your church would experience the tangible, unadulterated presence of God like never before.

How to Use It

This lesson series is meant to be a tool for you – whether you are a worship leader, worship pastor, or senior pastor – to use in making your worship rehearsals more significant than just a time to "woodshed" through songs. Those kind of rehearsals get old really quickly.

If you're like us, you really value your rehearsal time with your teams. We do not want to devalue the practical need of rehearsing songs. That is needed and important. However, this resource is meant to be a tool that enables you to pour into your team spiritually as well. It is when each member of the worship team connects the spiritual with the natural that your worship times really come alive.

Suggested Time Allotment:

We have specifically designed these lessons to be easily facilitated in as little as 15 minutes during your rehearsal. If you wish to go longer, we have experienced the reality that these lessons can easily last up to an hour, depending on how much your team "jumps in" on the discussion and prayer time.

Suggested Placement in the Rehearsal "Schedule":

The beauty about these lessons is that they can be done at *any* point during your rehearsal time. We have done them *before* we start musical rehearsal, in the *middle* of rehearsal (rehearse fast songs, break for the lesson, and then resume with the slower songs), and also at the *end* of rehearsal. There is much flexibility, so the choice is yours.

How Do I Teach It?

The lessons are in no particular order (other than the lessons named "Pt. 1" and "Pt. 2"). So, feel free to choose whatever lesson you'd like. The lessons are built for ease of instruction. We'll walk you through it:

> **Step 1**: Prior to the worship rehearsal, select the lesson you want to bring to the team.

Step 2: Log on to www.tfhworship.com and download the "Student Copy" of the lesson you are bringing to the team during rehearsal. The student copies have the fill-in-the-blanks that are highlighted in your copies (in this book).

Step 3: Simply read through the introductory section. This first portion of each chapter is a section written from us to you, highlighting important leadership aspects regarding the lesson."

Step 4: During the teaching portion of your worship rehearsal, read "**The Lesson**" to your team.

NOTE: The *underlined* portions in the lessons in this book are fill-in-the-blanks in the student copies.

Step 5: The "**Discussion**" section has several options for discussion questions. Pick a couple that you'd like to discuss with your team. If you want to do all of them, be our guest!

Step 6: Take time to pray over the subject matter using the "**Prayer Points**" section. Again, you may pick a couple prayer points you like, or you may pray over all of them.

Step 7: We always encourage our team to take the lessons home and continue to pray/read over the subject matter during the week before the worship service. This has a great unifying effect in the team before the weekend.

And that's it! Simple enough, isn't it? That's kind of how we wanted it to be. A simple way for you to bring worship-specific teachings to supplement your worship rehearsals. Have fun!

We believe in you, and we're praying for you.

Dave Patterson
Senior Pastor, The Father's House

Joseph Zwanziger
Worship Pastor, The Father's House

Chapter 1

Being a Gift

If you've been in ministry for very long at all, you probably already have a list of people who constantly drain your time. Either they do not show up on time or – even when they do – they do not come prepared and you have to spend even *more* time making up for his/her lack. There are too many people exhibiting this type of character and it's enough to make you go CRAZY in ministry.

Prov. 25:19 says "Confidence in an unfaithful man in time of trouble is like a bad tooth and a foot out of joint." Basically, you can't rely on unfaithful people. When you try to use them/put weight on them, it is a painful experience (ever experienced this?).

This lesson is a very significant one in the scope of dealing with "support" ministry. It deals with the fact that God has called those who support the Senior Pastor and other leadership to be a gift instead of the opposite. Support ministers should be those who bring a smile to the face of leadership and not be those who cause fear and trembling in the hearts of pastors and leaders.

This lesson can be a bit interesting to deliver because of the very nature of your position as the leader and the one delivering this lesson. My suggestion to you would be to demonstrate by using your own relationship to the Senior Pastor/elders/pastors and how you yourself are called to be a gift to them. Your team will "catch the drift" concerning their relationship to you.

If you are a Senior Pastor, then perhaps you may want to select a mature member of your team to bring this lesson and discuss your heart with them. Make sure the context of this lesson is his/her heart toward you, and then let them share out of their heart and experience with you. It may even be a good idea for you to not be in the room for this lesson, so it can be delivered more genuinely (so your team isn't thinking, "Well, you're the one TELLING us to be like this"). Make sense?

Ultimately, this lesson comes down to spiritual authority and your team falling into the boundaries and heart-posture required to achieve the blessings released through submission. This is not an authoritarian thing but rather an effort to release greater measures of the grace, favor, and blessing of the Lord into and through your team and church.

I. The Lesson

If we're truly honest with ourselves, there are people – yes, even in the Church – who demand of us a greater grace when dealing with them. There are those who take more of your energy than you want to give, whose personalities clash with yours, and those who would talk into the wee hours of the morning if you'd let them. These people are not bad, they just are not the kind of people you would spend every day with if you had the chance.

But then here we are – support leaders, worship ministers. The Bible refers to us as Levites (1 Pet. 2:9). There are many aspects of the Levites that are amazing to study as it relates to us as New Testament Levites, but the one we will look at here is our relationship to our Senior Pastor, pastors, and elders.

> "And I have given the Levites as a gift to Aaron and his sons from among the children of Israel..." Num. 8:19

God has called us to be "gifts" to our Senior Pastor, pastors, and elders (Aaron and his sons). What an interesting concept. What happens in you when you get a gift? Sometimes, you get a gift and you wish the gift hadn't been given to you in the first place. We're not talking about that kind of gift.

The kind of gift God wants us to be to our Senior Pastor, pastors, and elders, is a gift that...

1) Brings **_refreshing_** .

Your acts of faithfulness, submission, and selfless serving make ministry a little bit easier for your leaders. God has placed a large mantle of responsibility on their shoulders. When you come along side them and support them in what God has called them to do, you are a true gift.

2) **_Encourages_** .

What a blessing it is to your pastors and leaders when they see people coming around them to support and serve them as they serve the Lord. They have given their lives for the cause of Christ for your city/region. You are a blessing to them.

3) **_Pushes them onward_** .

It is easy for your Senior Pastor to take tasks upon him/herself that other people could do for them. You are the kind of gift God intended you to be when you recognize that God has given your Senior Pastor a specific calling and you begin to take on the routine tasks so that he/she can focus on that calling. Ultimately, it will lead to the entire church being led into a more effective place of ministry.

4) Doesn't **_murmur/complain_** .

We need to have the heart of Jonathan's armor bearer...

> *"Do what you think is best... I'm with you completely, whatever you decide"* (1 Sam. 14:7, NLT**).**

When we are given a task, given new direction, or undergoing change, our leaders need to know that our answer will always be, "Do what you think is best, I'm with you completely." A man/woman of God will not take advantage of that, but be *even more* sure of his/her actions knowing that you have this attitude.

5) Is ready, _**in season and out**_ .

David had many "mighty men" who were always ready and willing to serve, fight for, and do anything the king required of them. As stated in 2 Tim. 4:2, they were "ready in season and out of season." This means that, no matter whether we are scheduled to serve on a particular day or not, we should be ready and willing to do whatever is asked of us. One of the greatest gifts to a Senior Pastor or other leader is knowing that there is a person who will be ready for the unexpected, one who can be counted on in time of need.

So, are you one who brings a smile to the face of your Senior Pastor, pastors, and elders because you exhibit the qualities listed above? Or are you one who cannot be counted on because of a lack in these areas? When we are truly a "gift" to our pastors and leaders, we are helping to set into motion a force that is hard to stop. It is the Church of Jesus Christ functioning as it is was intended from the beginning of creation - a church that experiences the blessings, favor, and power of God through proper submission to and honor of spiritual authority.

II. Discussion

1) What happens in a church when the Senior Pastor, pastors, or elders are left to run after the vision of God for your church on their own?
2) What are some of the ways that you can practically be a "gift" to your...
   a. Senior Pastor?
   b. Elders?
   c. Pastors?
   d. Worship Leader(s)?

3) What are the spiritual byproducts in the church when support ministry (i.e. the worship ministry) embraces their role as "gifts" and operates as such?
4) What are the tangible, natural byproducts in the church when support ministry (i.e. the worship ministry) embraces their role as "gifts" and operates as such?

III. Prayer Points

1) Pray that God would unify the worship team around the goal of being true "gifts" to the Senior Pastor, pastors, and elders of the church.
2) Pray that your leaders would be refreshed as they devote their lives to seeing the vision of God for your church come to pass.
3) Pray that God would equip you and give you the grace and strength to be ready "in season and out of season" – whether to step into new areas of ministry, new levels in the worship ministry, or whatever else may be asked of you individually.

Chapter 2

Coming Into His Presence – Pt.1
Thanksgiving

When I first began to lead worship (Joseph writing), my question was, "There has GOT to be some formula for this!" My cry was innocent, my heart was, "God, how can we consistently come into Your presence so we can experience Your goodness and lives will be changed forever?!"

It didn't take long for me to understand that there is truly no formula that is as simple as: Play this, then that, wear this, raise your hands like that. But as I have stuck with the awesome ministry of leading people into His presence; as I've pressed into the study of His Word, and as I've seen the application of His word in our churches, I've found that there truly is a "formula," a prescription that God gives us for entering His presence.

In this lesson we'll look at the first part of this "formula" which is thanksgiving. What a simple and yet profound concept. This concept of thanksgiving can be so difficult for musicians, though.

Musicians and singers are sensitive people. We're *emotional* people. Those emotions can help us relate to and communicate the things of God to His people in unique and effective ways. They can also serve as a hindrance to effective ministry if we're not careful.

As we talk about in the chapter "Culture of Joy," we work very hard with the musicians and singers at our church to "stir up" joy and thanksgiving before every service. In His presence, there is fullness of joy! So musicians and singers who carry depression, doubt, worry, and anxiety to the platform are bringing issues that act as *barriers* we must bring down in order to really enter the presence of God.

Although it seems trivial, as a leader, you MUST guard the spirit of your team. Psalm 100 tells us that the first protocol for entering the presence of God is to enter with thanksgiving.

I. The Lesson

Have you ever been frustrated with experiences in your worship services where one week feels like you're caught up into the third heaven and the next week you question your salvation due to the seeming lack of the presence of God? Have you ever wondered, "Is there some kind of formula for consistently getting into the presence of God?"

There are many different variables that play a part in the perceived level of the presence of God in our services: The level of faith/expectancy of the people in the congregation, our personal holiness, technical considerations, etc. However, the Word shows us a very important principle regarding entering the presence of God. It is fail-safe. It works every time. It is as simple as... thanksgiving – no, not the holiday, the heart condition and expression.

"Enter into His gates with thanksgiving..." Psalm 100:4

The first instruction in this protocol of entering His presence (His gates) is to enter with thanksgiving. Let's look at what this word means.

Thanksgiving = ***towdah*** (heb.) = ___*lifting of our hands*___ .
= ___*giving thanks*___ to Him.

We give thanks to God for...
1) ___*Who*___ He is (Savior, Healer, Redeemer, Comforter, etc.)
2) ___*What*___ He's done for us (cleansed us, saved us, given us access to His presence, etc.)
3) Who ___*we are*___ in Him (victorious, righteous, cleansed, etc.)
4) ___*What*___ He's *going* to do, etc.

We have SO MUCH to be thankful for. When we, as His people, come to Him with thanksgiving in our hearts, lifting our hands, expressing our thanks to Him, He cannot stay away! He has purposed it in His heart to draw near to us when we draw near to Him (James 4:8). In the context of worship, this happens when we draw near to Him with a heart of thanksgiving.

It is important to understand that if God draws near to a heart of thanksgiving, He draws *away* from hearts of murmuring and complaining. Perhaps this is why we fail to enter into His tangible, manifest presence on a consistent basis. When the children of Israel murmured and complained in the desert, things didn't turn out so great.

How do we "stir up" thanksgiving?

The language of thanksgiving is __***found in the Word***__ .

> Psalm 95:2 *"Let us come before him with "thanksgiving" and extol him with music and song."*

> Psalm 107:21-22 *"Oh, that men would give thanks to the Lord for His goodness, and for His wonderful works to the children of men! Let them sacrifice the sacrifices of "thanksgiving", and declare His works with rejoicing."*

> Psalm 116:17 *"I will offer to You the sacrifice of "thanksgiving", and will call upon the name of the Lord."*

So encourage one another and stir up thanksgiving in your team. Your example will lead your congregation into new places in worship and the presence of God.

II. Discussion

1) What are some of the reasons that we, as musicians and singers, struggle with consistently bringing a heart of thanksgiving?

2) What are the byproducts of musicians and singers who do NOT bring a heart and countenance of thanksgiving on a weekly basis (both on the team and the congregation)?
3) How can we, as a team, "stir up" thanksgiving in ourselves and each other?
4) How can we help the congregation grow in this aspect of bringing a heart of thanksgiving to every service?

III. Prayer Points

1) Pray for an increase of thanksgiving in our lives, individually and as a team.
2) Pray for protection over the worship ministry... the enemy would LOVE to attack the worship team's thanksgiving.
3) Pray that the bondages of depression, anxiety, and anything else that would hinder our joy would be broken.
4) Pray that God would give us hearts of thanksgiving, that we'd look for things to be thankful for more than we look for things to be upset about.

Chapter 3

Coming Into His Presence – Pt.2
With Praise

We talked in "Coming Into His Presence – Pt. 1" about how thanksgiving is the first requirement of entering the presence of the Lord. Thanksgiving stands contrary to depression, self-absorbency, and everything else that emotional musician-types can fall into and hinder our freedom in worship.

In this lesson, we will discuss the second ingredient: Praise. As a worship ministry, we've always been very careful about the songs we choose. There are many songs in the worship "market" today that speak *about* God, but we want to focus on the ones where we sing *to* God. It may sound like a subtle difference, but the Word tells us that when we lift our praise *to* Him, He is "enthroned" on it and His presence fills the house. We will also talk about praise that is spontaneous, fresh, and straight from our hearts. Singing songs that are written are good, but the key to the praise that God "inhabits" is that it is an unwritten song.

We encourage you to point out the subtleties in this lesson to your team. Explain the philosophy of directing our praise *to* God and what it leads to. "Let them in on" the vision and the theology of worship that you as their leader and the leadership of the church are embracing. This will serve to help your team's worship to be faith-filled and purposeful.

I. The Lesson

In the previous lesson on "Coming Into His Presence," we talked about how thanksgiving is the first part of the "formula" for coming into

God's presence, both on a personal and congregational level. While thanksgiving is powerful in itself, it is important that we do not miss the second requirement for coming into His presence: Praise.

> *"Enter... into His courts with praise."* Psalm 100:4

Praise means different things to different people. Even in the Hebrew language that the Psalms were originally written in, there are many different words for praise. The word for praise in this passage is **Tehillah**.

Tehillah = ___**spontaneous**___ praise

= praise offered from our ___**hearts**___ , not from words on a screen

The picture, historically, is very vivid as well. When Israel would set up the Tabernacle of Moses in the desert, the tribes of Israel would have to set up camp surrounding the Tabernacle (representing the presence of God). The tribe that camped right outside the entrance to the Tabernacle was the tribe of Judah. Judah means praise. See where we're going with this? In order to get into the Tabernacle (the presence of God), you would literally have to walk through "praise" (Judah)! (see diagram below)

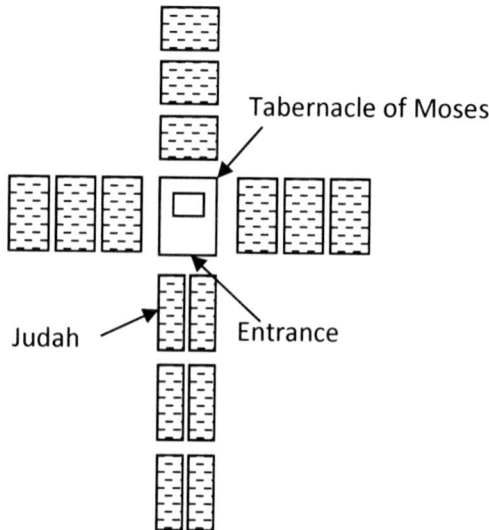

Tabernacle of Moses

Judah   Entrance

It is the same way for us today. It is not good enough to just play great songs, sing every note accurately, and pray before service. All that is great, but God has given us an outline in His Word. We enter His gates with thanksgiving and His courts with praise!

Let's look at another promise in Psalms regarding this *tehillah* (spontaneous) praise.

> *"But You are holy, enthroned in the praises of Israel"* Psalm 22:3

Israel represents the people of God – the Church. The Hebrew word for praise here, once again, is *tehillah* – spontaneous, from-the-heart praise. When we offer God this kind of praise, He is enthroned upon it. This means that He makes the place where this praise is offered His **_habitation_** – He sets up His throne there!. What does this mean?

- God chooses to **_dwell_** in our praise.

- If His throne is established, other "thrones" are **_torn down_**.
    Freedom replaces bondage.
    Joy replaces depression.
    Healing replaces sickness.
    Wholeness replaces brokenness.

What an amazing environment! Who wouldn't want to be a part of this? It's not some ethereal thing either. It is unlocked by worship teams and worshipers who enter His presence with thanksgiving and praise. What an awesome privilege! What an awesome opportunity!

II. Discussion
1) What are some of the ways we, as worshipers, can become more comfortable with singing spontaneous praise to the Lord?
2) What are the implications, musically, of taking time to sing spontaneously to the Lord? (What do we do musically?)

3) What can we, as a worship team, do to encourage our congregation to offer this kind of praise in our worship services?

4) If we, as a worship team and a church, never sang praise *to* God, but rather *about* God, what affect would that have on worship experience of our church?

III. Prayer Points

1) Pray for freedom over the worship team and congregation to step out and purposefully lift spontaneous praise to the Lord.

2) Pray that the worship level of the church would begin to mature as a whole – that our level of praise would not waiver as different seasons of life occur.

3) Pray that the manifest presence of God would increase in our worship times… that the things discussed in this lesson would be a consistent reality in our church.

Chapter 4

Countenance

One of the most eye-opening experiences for you as a leader is to review a video recording of you and your team leading the congregation into worship on any given weekend. Truly, to be a team that is effective in leading people into worship, attention must be given to not only how you sound, but how you look on stage.

What we have found is that, as leaders, it's easy to focus so much on getting the sound to be right – the drums and bass grooving, the guitars and pianos living in harmony, and our three-part harmonies in perfect sync – that we forget about how we look, specifically our countenance (we refer to it at our church as being "models of worship"). It's also true that when we mess up on stage in some way, a very small percentage of the congregation can actually tell that we messed up, while we beat ourselves up off stage for every little mistake.

Although musical excellence plays a big part in leading people into the presence of God in worship, what many leaders/teams fail to realize is that our countenance on stage is HUGE as far as motivating the congregation to worship. If our teams hit every note perfectly but look bored, annoyed, or uninterested on stage, it sends a message to the congregation – even if the band is truly well-intentioned.

For instance; think about the background vocalist who is legitimately trying to meet with God. Her voice is spot on, hands are raised, gentle swaying motion side-to-side... but the expression on her face looks like she just dropped a hammer on her toe! Come on, you know what I'm talking about. If you don't, then just take a look at a video recording of this next weekend and you'll see it!

This lesson is vitally important for the life of our worship times. If we look like we're having a good time on stage, meeting with God, overflowing with joy in the process, then our congregation is likely to experience the same. We encourage you to approach this lesson with your team in a lighthearted and gracious manner. Expose the error in your ways as a team, but offer the hope of, "Let's all help each other in this and keep each other accountable week-to-week with our countenance." It may be painful, initially, but it will do wonders for your church in the long-run. We encourage you to pick up DVDs of examples of how countenance is done well (e.g. Hillsong Australia, Desperation Band, Israel Houghton, etc.) and show them along with this lesson.

I. The Lesson

We all understand that in order to be an effective worship team, we need to practice regularly in order to ensure that everyone is on the "same page" musically. We know that the more musical skill we have, the better we'll be able to inspire people into a place of worship with God. We even see how the Bible repeatedly places value on excellence in ministry (for us, it's musical... see "Musical Excellence"). However, there is one aspect of our role as worship ministers that usually gets overlooked by the majority of worship teams. A lack of appropriate execution of this element can immediately hinder the effectiveness of the musical element we worked so hard to produce. Pop stars call it "stage presence." We call it "countenance."

Webster's Dictionary defines countenance as a "look or expression." Therefore, our countenance involves everything from the clothes we wear to the look on our face to our body movements while on stage.

We can play every note correctly, sing every melody and harmony with precision, and nail every solo and feature, but if our countenance is not aligning with the declaration we're singing, the congregation will be confused, unmotivated, and have the sense of, "I'm not buying it."

So, we must give careful consideration to how we look on stage. We're not talking about a vain thought of, "Is my hair okay?" but rather, "Is what I'm doing right now inspiring people to worship?" If we're singing about how good God is, yet we look like our dog just died right before we got on stage, there is an obvious inconsistency that must be addressed.

Through studying the Psalms (and seen throughout scripture), we see nine expressions God commanded us (through David) to use in praise and worship. Those expressions are...

Using our Hands:
1) __*Clapping*__ .   2) __*Lifting*__ .   3) __*Playing Instruments*__ .

Using our Voice:
1) __*Singing*__ .   2) __*Speaking*__ .   3) __*Shouting*__ .

Using our Posture:
1) __*Standing*__ .   2) __*Bowing/Kneeling.*__ 3) __*Dancing*__ .

Since God has commanded us throughout scripture to praise Him in these ways, then we – as the worship ministers and "models of worship" – must demonstrate these forms to the congregation. We frequently encourage our teams...

"What happens on stage is contagious in the congregation"

This is true in more than just with countenance, but if we – as the worship team – are demonstrating these various forms of praising God, we are in a sense saying to the congregation, "Do as we do," and people will catch on.

Part of this issue of whether we do or do not exemplify a proper worship countenance is our heart attitude.

Rom. 12:11 *"... Serve the Lord enthusiastically."* (NLT)

1 Cor. 15:58 *"...Always work enthusiastically for the Lord." (NLT)*

How do we work and serve the Lord enthusiastically while on the platform? By demonstrating the nine expressions of worship. "But what if I don't *feel* like it? Do it anyway! It's your JOB as a worship minister. If we always wait until we *feel* like worshiping, we probably wouldn't worship that often (if we're brutally honest). But if we worship because we know it's the best thing for us, that He is worthy of our offering, and God is seeking worshipers (John 4:23-24), we will worship *no matter what*!

> It is easier to act your way into feelings
> than it is to feel your way into actions.

So, approach the platform every time you minister with an attitude that is set on musical excellence and a countenance that models enthusiastic service unto the Lord. *That* is the picture of an effective worship minister.

The following are some good questions to ask yourself regarding countenance:

- Am I ___ *smiling* ___? Do I look like I'm enjoying myself and God?

- Is my ___ *attire* ___ "tastefully contributing to a low profile?"[1]

- Do my ___ *emotions* ___ reflect the "emotion" of the song/what's going on?

---

[1] Sorge, Bob. Exploring Worship: A Practical Guide to Praise & Worship. Pg. 158. 1987, 2001. Oasis House. Lee's Summit, Missouri.

II. Discussion

1) As a worship team, what are we doing well in the area of countenance?
2) As a worship team, how can we improve in the area of countenance?
3) If we are not enthusiastic on stage, what does that portray to the congregation?
4) What effect does a worship team who is not enthusiastic have on the spiritual atmosphere of the service?
5) What are ways that singers can demonstrate the nine expressions of Psalmic praise and worship? Guitarists? Drummers? Keyboardists? Etc...

III. Prayer Points

1) Pray that God would refresh each member of the team and that we would look forward to ministering, not dread it.
2) Pray that God would give us grace, as a worship team, to have the boldness required to demonstrate Biblical expressions of praise.
3) Pray that there would be freedom released in the congregation to join in enthusiastic worship with us as we experience that freedom.

Chapter 5

Creating a Culture of Joy

Artist-types are very unique. We are very sensitive, emotional, and creative. Those attributes provide many good things, but they are also accompanied by some issues that need to be dealt with. As far as this lesson goes, we're going to focus on the issue of joy and its antitheses: sorrow, anguish, depression, and distress.

The issue of coming to minister "full of joy" is vitally important. Watching a depressed person on stage will never produce a heart of worship in others. It is very important that we, as leaders, work to preserve a spirit of joy in our teams. Now, we understand that life happens and people go through hard times. However, if this affects a person's ability to minister effectively (see "Countenance"), then that person should be temporarily removed from the team.

It is a JOYOUS thing to be in the House of God, in the presence of a Holy God, to minister to Him and to His people. This is the attitude we must share as a worship team. We're not here to sing the blues, we're here to minister hope and faith and healing to the Body of Christ. We cannot effectively do this if we ourselves are feeling just the opposite.

In our worship ministry, we have intentionally set out to "create a culture of joy" in our team and, as a team, we in turn intentionally set out to "create a culture of joy" in the congregation. We encourage you to do the same. Encourage your teams to pour out their hearts to the Lord in their own times and deal with the issues of life in the secret place. Then, come to minister full of joy and ready to minister that joy to the congregation.

II. The Lesson

Let's not be naive; sometimes we really don't feel like ministering on any particular weekend. There are times when we are physically tired, exhausted, or sick; we're dealing with issues in our lives that contend for our focus and attention; we are discouraged; or perhaps, for whatever reason, we feel spiritually empty (can come from a lack of spending time in the secret place).

As worship ministers, it is important to understand that it is *vitally important that we minister from a place of joy.* Consider the following scriptures:

Psalm 16:11 *"In Your presence is fullness of joy"*

Psalm 100:2 *"Worship the* LORD *with gladness. Come before Him, singing with joy."*

- Joy is a **_prerequisite_** for coming before the Lord

Isaiah 35:10 *"And the ransomed of the* LORD *will return.* **They will enter Zion with singing**; *everlasting joy will crown their heads.* **Gladness and joy will overtake them,** *and sorrow and sighing will flee away."*

Isaiah 56:7 *"I will bring them to my holy mountain of Jerusalem and* **will fill them with joy in my house of prayer."**

John 15:10-11 *"When you obey my commandments, you remain in my love, just as I obey my Father's commandments and remain in his love.* [11]*I have told you these things so that you will be filled with my joy. Yes,* **your joy will overflow!"**

Remaining in His ___*love*___ and doing His ___*will*___ results in JOY.

Neh. 8:10 *"Don't be dejected and sad, for **the joy of the LORD is your strength**!"*

It is God's design that our times of corporate worship are times that are full of joy! These are times of celebration of what the Lord has done in and through us as believers and as a Body. As we worship, His promise is that we will be "overtaken" by gladness and joy. It is this joy that is the source of our strength as the people of God.

It should not come as a great surprise to us, then, that one of the main areas the enemy tries to attack is our joy.

No joy = no strength

As worship ministers, it is vitally important that we guard our joy, come to minister full of joy, and minister out of joy to intentionally create a culture of joy in our congregation. When you really think about it, how many people in any given service are coming in sad, dejected, depressed, maybe even suicidal? - pretty much anything but joyful. It is a reality we need to face.

Another reality is the fact that there are those who come to church and aren't happy about it, whether they had a bad experience in the past or have never really understood that church is a JOYFUL experience. We get to model the reality of the fullness of JOY in the presence of the Lord.

There is a great exchange that happens in the presence of the Lord (see Isaiah 61:3):

God Gives	In Exchange For
**Beauty**	Ashes
Oil of Joy	Mourning
**Praise**	Heaviness

Our joy, as worship ministers, also springs from the revelation that we're a part of God's plan to minister to His people and extend His Kingdom in the earth.

> *"For no matter how significant you are, it is only because of what you are a part of."* 1 Cor. 12:20 (MSG)

We are a part of something great. Let's go after joy with a new fervency!

"There is nothing like the local church... its beauty is indescribable. Its power is breathtaking. Its potential is unlimited. It comforts the grieving and heals the broken in the context of community. It builds bridges to seekers and offers truth to the confused. It provides resources for those in need and opens its arms to the forgotten, the downtrodden, the disillusioned. It breaks the chains of addictions, frees the oppressed, and offers belonging to the marginalized of this world. Whatever the capacity for human suffering, the church has a greater capacity for healing and wholeness."[2]

---

[2] Hybels, Bill. Courageous Leadership. Pg. 23, 2002. Zondervan. Grand Rapids, Michigan

II. Discussion

1) What can we do as individuals to increase our joy?
2) What are some of the main ways our joy is attacked as worship ministers?
3) What are the byproducts in the congregation when a worship team is not joyful on stage?
4) How can we, as a worship team, encourage each other in the area of our "joy level?"

III. Prayer Points

1) Pray for an increase of the fruit of the Spirit in the lives of each member of the worship team (one fruit is *joy* – Gal. 5:22).
2) Pray for an increase of the presence of the Lord in your services... In His presence is "fullness of joy."
3) Pray that the joy of the Lord would be on His people; that depression, anxiety, fear, disappointment, and every other thing that suppresses joy in them would be suffocated in joy.

Chapter 6

Creating a Prophetic Atmosphere

DISCLAIMER: For some, "Creating a prophetic atmosphere" might be a pretty scary title. In case you are reading this teaching and are not accustomed to using terms like "prophetic worship" or a "prophetic gathering," allow me to disarm any apprehension by giving you a workable definition of "prophetic worship":

> Moving prophetically in worship is to move with an awareness of the desire and leading of the Holy Spirit moment by moment.

An extended definition is: to discern the direction of the Spirit and to participate in it; walking and talking with the Lord (Genesis 3:8-9) not only to speak, but also to listen and respond to the Word and direction of the Lord.

The goal of this lesson is to introduce – or heighten the awareness – of our role in creating an atmosphere where people can hear from God. This happens as the worship team learns to make a place for the voice of God to be heard and makes a place for the spontaneous, God-inspired moments that turn a worship set into an encounter.

The ramifications of prophetic worship for the pastors and worship leaders are great blessings mixed with potential dangers and problems that arise whenever we move into uncharted waters with people who are inevitably going to make mistakes. The blessings are the excitement, refreshing, and life that are released when our worship times are visited with the unpredictable. Just remember, the blessings far outweigh the problems and every move of the spirit requires pastors and leaders who are able to guide and guard the people of God.

There is no chapter and verse on exactly how this should look or be administrated in the worship services that we lead. First Corinthians 14 is the closest set of guidelines that we have when it comes to determining what is fitting and in order. So, please explore this topic without a sense of pressure or condemnation, knowing that God has called you and your worship team to develop a unique expression of worship in your community.

I. The Lesson

Releasing a prophetic atmosphere in our worship services is really about faith and awareness: faith that God desires and will in fact speak to His people as we worship Him and awareness as the Holy Spirit leads us . True worship is never one-sided and always involves interaction with the Holy Spirit. Jesus said:
"My sheep hear My voice, and I know them, and they follow Me" (John 10:27).

His voice can be heard anytime, anywhere, but is most consistently and accurately discerned in the context of worship. When people sense God, hear from God, and meet with God during worship, it has the potential to change them for eternity. That is why so many people connect their worship experience to particular songs that have an emotional or nostalgic appeal – they simply met with and heard from God while certain songs were being sung!

How do we Create a Prophetic Atmosphere ?

1) Realize that creating an atmosphere where the voice of God is heard is an act of __*faith*__!

Heb. 11:6 *"Without faith it is impossible to please God, because anyone who comes to him must believe that he exists and that he rewards those who earnestly seek him."*

It doesn't take faith to perform worship songs. It doesn't take faith to sing tenor, play an instrument, or run a sound board. But it does take faith to believe that the singing of songs, playing of instruments, and operating of technical equipment will actually bring a change to the atmosphere that enables people to connect with the Living God.

2) Make a place for the __**spontaneous**__ and unpredictable.

When we take the spontaneous and supernatural conversation out of our worship, it becomes dead liturgy! Even if it's contemporary and 102 decibels, without the divine interaction of God's voice, worship times will always be reduced to a formula, a song list, or a religious form that we refine and repeat. What we desire in our worship is the life, excitement, and anticipation that comes when people are hearing from and meeting with God! This prophetic atmosphere was a consistent element in the New Testament Church and is still available today.

> 1 Cor. 14:26 "What then shall we say, brothers? When you come together, everyone has a hymn, or a word of instruction, a revelation, a tongue or an interpretation. All of these must be done for the strengthening of the church."
> Acts 13:2 "While they were worshiping the Lord and fasting, the Holy Spirit said..."

3) Create __*a throne*__ for the Lord.

As we truly praise, the atmosphere is changed and God is enthroned. Our heart-felt expressions of worship literally set up a zone of God's authority and His kingdom is established on earth. When we realize the power and significance of this one principle, it can change the way we view our role on the worship team as well as the way we approach the precious moments when we come together for our worship times.

> Psalm 22:3 *"But You are holy, Who inhabit the praises of Israel."*

Praise (*tehillah*): laudation; the words of the *halal* melodiously chanted; spontaneous in nature (the song of the Spirit)

2 Chr. 31:2 *"Hezekiah **assigned the priests and Levites** to divisions -each of them according to their duties as priests or Levites - to offer burnt offerings and fellowship offerings, to minister, to give thanks and to **sing praises at the gates of the LORD'S dwelling**."*

4) Understand and release the ministry of the __*minstrel*__ .

> **Minstrel** / *Nagan* = To play or pluck a stringed instrument, to beat a tune with the fingers; to make music
>
> **Worship minstrel:** One who plays an instrument and releases the presence of God.

2 Kings 13:14-*16 "Elisha said, 'As surely as the LORD Almighty lives, whom I serve, if I did not have respect for the presence of Jehoshaphat king of Judah, I would not look at you or even notice you.* [15] *But now bring me a harpist (minstrel).' **While the minstrel was playing**, the hand of the LORD came upon Elisha* [16] *and he said, 'This is what the LORD says...'"*

1 Chr. 25:1 *"Moreover David and the captains of the army separated for the service some of the sons of Asaph, of Heman, and of Jeduthun, who should **prophesy with** harps, stringed instruments, and cymbals."* see (Isaiah 30:27)

5) ___*Intentionally*___ create "the watercourse" (rivers of instrumental worship).

Gen. 4:21 *"His brother's name was Jubal. He was the father of all those who play the harp and flute."*

> **Jubal** / *Yuwba* = to create a stream; to bring or cause a flow.

Psalm 46:4 *"There is a river whose **streams** make glad the city of God, the holy place where the Most High dwells."*

"There is a river whose tributaries bring joy to the divine city" [Har] (see John 7:38)

6) Eliminate __*distractions*__!
This teaching does not just apply to those on stage who are singing, speaking, or playing. It actually applies to everyone from the parking lot to the nursery and beyond! Let's look at one example. Let's say a church uses lighting and visual effects to enhance the worship experience. If the lighting and camera people are not sensitive and consciously involved in creating the atmosphere, they can become more of a hindrance than a blessing.

II. Discussion

1) How would you define "spontaneous moments" in worship? How often do you experience them?
2) What are some blessings as well as potential dangers that are released when we make room for "prophetic worship"? *(refer to definition)*
3) What would be the difference between a good musician and a "prophetic minstrel?"
4) How do we intentionally create a flow of instrumental worship? What are some ways the "flow" is interrupted?
5) How do lighting engineers, sound engineers, ushers, camera people, and all other servants in the meeting influence the atmosphere? Both positive and negative examples will be profitable to discuss.

III. Prayer Points

1) Pray for sensitivity and awareness of the leading of the Holy Spirit for every worship time.

2) Ask for, long for, and earnestly desire the gifts of the Spirit to operate in the gatherings of God's people:

   1 Cor. 12:31 *"But earnestly desire the best gifts."*
   1 Cor. 14:1 *"Pursue love, and desire spiritual gifts, but especially that you may prophesy."*

3) Pray for a brand new level of faith and expectancy that God will meet with you as you intentionally make new places for His voice to be heard during worship.
4) Pray for the anointing and wisdom to be psalmists and minstrels, not just musicians.
5) Ask the Lord to make your place of worship a place where people meet with, hear from, and are radically changed by God... every week!

Chapter 7

Excellence

There is a fine line that separates excellence and perfectionism. Excellence reflects the heart of God, while perfectionism is a dangerous trap to fall into that can tear apart worship ministries.

In this lesson, we will look at this highly debated topic, "Excellence." There are many different thoughts and practices when it comes to excellence in churches all over the globe. The continuum of excellence reaches the extremes, from perfectionism to complete disregard.

In our church, we hold a high standard for excellence with the end goal of bringing the best offering to God that we can, whether it be the quality of our music or the quality of the cleaning of the bathrooms. Excellence is applicable across all areas of the church but none are more debated than in regard to worship ministry (music, lighting, media, etc.).

It is important for you as the leader to understand that you will come under fire from those who do not have an accurate theology of excellence and its role in the church. You will be accused of being a perfectionist. You will be accused of not seeking the heart of God but of seeking perfection in the services.

That's the nitty-gritty. The great thing about your role is that you get to motivate your team toward excellence, with the end result of glorifying God in and through it. In every temple, tabernacle, and tent where God was honored in the Bible, every element was executed in excellence. It was that excellence that God would anoint and move upon/through. Don't you want that to be your church?

It will be important to encourage your team toward excellence and not "beat them over the head" for not being excellent. You want to motivate, not discourage. Remember, excellent musicians are attracted to excellent musicians. Excellence *IS* achievable no matter what the resource level is that you have in your church. **Go after it!**

I. The Lesson

Have you ever walked into a worship service (maybe at your church, perhaps at another church or conference) and were so blown away by the band, lighting, music, sound, and/or media elements that it drew you into a place of worship like a magnet? It has been demonstrated throughout the Bible and history how excellence in what we do creates an atmosphere of worship that is irresistible to worshipers and to God.

Excellence has been a hotly debated issue in the church, especially in recent years as more technology has enabled the local church to do more during services. In this lesson, we will look at what God thinks/feels about excellence as well as our response to the call to excellence.

Somewhere along the line, some churchgoers got it in their minds that great musicianship or vocal ability, video screens, moving lights, well-planned and executed sound reinforcement, and well-planned song lists were not only not necessary but they were distractions that have no place in church. While the above mentioned items can be carried out in a way that could be distracting and might not be done for the right reasons, excellence in the House of God is nothing new.

Excellence throughout the Bible

> Lev. 1:3, 9 *"Let him offer a male **without blemish**... And the priest shall burn all on the altar as a burnt sacrifice, an offering made by fire, a **sweet aroma to the L*ORD*.*"

The Lord commanded Moses to tell the people of God that their worship (offerings) should be excellent. This excellent offering was a sign of people giving their __*best*__ to God. It was the people giving the best they could of what they had. They could not bring the lame, maimed, or diseased sheep or goat that would die anyway. Who would want that? Their excellent offering was a pleasing sacrifice to God. Likewise, when we bring our best to God in worship (musically, technically, attitudes, etc.), it is a pleasing aroma to God.

> 2 Chr. 2:13-14 *"And now I have sent a **skillful** man, **endowed with understanding**… **skilled** to work in gold and silver, bronze and iron, stone and wood, purple and blue, fine linen and crimson, and to make any engraving and to accomplish any plan which may be given to him, with your **skillful men** and with the **skillful men** of my lord David your father."*

Even the preparation of the House of God was carried out with excellence in the Old Testament. The above reference was during the building of Solomon's temple. The temple was so amazing in its completion that kings and queens would come from far off just to see it. Later, in 2 Chronicles 5, after the entire temple had been built with excellence, God's presence came so heavily, no one could stand under the weight of it! One of the primary factors in the Lord's coming was the excellence that was offered in the project.

Notice that it was said that the skillful worker could "accomplish any plan which may be given to him." When we work toward bringing excellence "to the table," we can be used for any plan given to us. When our skill is limited, so is our usability. **We should strive for excellence so that we may be ready "to accomplish any plan" which God may have for us**.

> Psalm 33:3 *"Sing to Him a new song; **Play skillfully** with a shout of joy."*

Psalm 47:7 *"For God is the King of all the earth; **Sing praises with a skillful psalm**."*

As if the examples weren't proof enough, over and over we are __*commanded*__ in the Word to offer God a skillful/excellent offering. Does God accept a musician/singer who maybe isn't the most talented person in the world? Of course. However, an offering that is excellent, "Without defect" brings honor and glory to God. Essentially, we are saying, "Lord, You are worthy of the very *best* I can bring You."

> When we operate in excellence, we are reflecting the nature and characteristics of the God Who does everything with excellence.

Excellence Leads To:

1) __*Freedom*__ in Worship

Let's face it, there is nothing easy about worshiping with horrible music. When the music and presentation are done with excellence, it provides an unparalleled freedom in worship for the congregation.

2) Increased __*Expression*__ in Worship

When we bring an excellent "offering" as worship musicians/singers, there are more "tools" we have to use in worship to respond to where God is leading us. Excellence allows us to better respond during spontaneous moments in worship and to better execute more difficult songs which may be a different genre than what we are used to.

3) __*Unity*__ Within the Worship Team

Musical unity is a result of each musician and singer bringing musical excellence in what they do. Ask any secular band. There is synergy that is created when the musicians are in unity.   That only happens through excellence.

4) People Being ___*Drawn*___ to Worship

Refer to the opening illustration of this lesson. Excellence draws people into the presence of God. People want to be a part of something excellent. Add the fact that God loves to be a part of something excellent, and you have an *electric* atmosphere in your church!

Psalm 66:2 *"Sing out the honor of His name; Make His praise glorious."*

II. Discussion

1) What keeps you from going after excellence with your instrument/voice personally?
2) What happens in a church when all areas of ministry are carried out with excellence?
3) What happens if only a few members of the worship team go after excellence, but not all?
4) How can we, as a worship team, work toward bringing an excellent offering, week after week?
5) What are some potential traps we could fall into in our pursuit of excellence?

III. Prayer Points

1) Pray that God would forgive us for ever thinking we are "good enough" to be on the worship team. He is worthy of the best we can bring Him.
2) Pray that God would give us the grace to go after excellence every week.
3) Pray for the congregation, that they would experience the byproducts of excellence and learn to embrace it in all areas of their lives.

4) Pray that God would continually reveal areas to us where we need to "step it up" in our level of commitment and our diligence to bring an excellent offering.

Chapter 8

Musical Preparation

~~~◦◦◦◦◦~~~

We probably don't have to tell you (as a leader) how frustrating it is when your musicians or singers do not come to rehearsal or service prepared musically. Your "success" in the worship service is largely determined by the preparation of the musicians. This preparation is both short-term and long-term.

In this lesson, we will discuss some very basic principles regarding preparation. For too long, worship team members have carried an attitude that "I'm good *enough* to play on the worship team," and so they do not practice or take the time to really study effective worship music.

One thing I tell new musicians and singers (Joseph speaking) is that worship music is not just "rock 'n roll for Jesus." It is its own style of music, with its own rules, just like any other genre of music.

Through this lesson, encourage and motivate your team to pursue preparation with a new vigor. Encourage them to break off the numb response to worship ministry that is all too often demonstrated by musicians who never pick up their instruments during the week and singers who never perfect and strengthen their vocal ability.

I. The Lesson

If you have ever taken formal musical lessons of any kind, one of the most dreaded words to hear is "practice." Practice takes diligence. Practice is rarely fun. However, practice is absolutely necessary in our pursuit of bringing God an excellent offering (see "Excellence"). Lucky for you, this entire lesson is NOT about practice. It is, however, about preparation.

Have you ever watched really high-level musicians perform? There is a seeming ease in their playing or singing. They seem effortless. Although there is an inherent amount of natural gift resident in them, great musicians and singers have learned that preparation is key to successful performances.

Although we are not performing for an audience when we are in worship services, we *are* performing for an "audience of One." How much more important is it that we practice and prepare for our performance/ministry before Him? While many secular musicians and singers perform for money and selfish motives, we get to minister to Him, minister to His people, and see God do amazing things through His church!

Let's look at one of the clearest examples in the Bible of how preparation led to an amazing move of God!

Second Chronicles chapters two through four detail the preparation put into the building of Solomon's Temple. The best materials were used by the best craftsmen in its construction. Solomon stopped at no length to build the house of God. After construction was complete, we see an account of the dedication of the temple – what a day it was.

> 2 Chr. 5:11-14 *"¹¹And it came to pass when the priests came out of the Most Holy Place (for all the priests who were present had sanctified themselves, without keeping to their divisions), ¹²and the Levites who were the singers, all those of Asaph and Heman and Jeduthun, with their sons and their brethren, stood at the east end of the altar, clothed in white linen, having cymbals, stringed instruments and harps, and with them one hundred and twenty priests sounding with trumpets— ¹³indeed it came to pass, when the trumpeters and singers were as one, to make one sound to be heard in praising and thanking the Lord, and when they lifted up their voice with the trumpets and cymbals and*

instruments of music, and praised the LORD, *saying: 'For He is good, For His mercy endures forever,' that the house, the house of the* LORD, *was filled with a cloud, [14]so that the priests could not continue ministering because of the cloud; for the glory of the* LORD *filled the house of God."*

What an amazing event to be a part of. We all want God to move in our church in this powerful way, right? This passage (and countless others) show the direct relationship between preparation and the power of God being released in a given environment. **God anoints preparation!**

Preparation in the local church goes way beyond the preparation required of the worship team, but we will focus there for the purpose of this lesson.

Areas of Preparation for Worship Ministry Members

1) ___*Musical Study*___ .

Our "continuing education" as musicians and singers happens through private lessons, musical classes at a local community college/junior college, or other venue. Professional musicians will tell you that they **never stop learning**.

2) ___*Rehearsal*___ .

This is not referring to attending worship rehearsals **only**, but also rehearsing specific parts on your own time. This rehearsal time promotes excellence among the team, and has the natural and supernatural result of drawing people into worship.

3) ___*Instrument Care*___ .

What good is it to work on a part for eight hours and come to service and have a broken string on your guitar or broken drum sticks? Whatever the case may be, you have to prepare your instrument for use as well as you prepare for your own musical performance.

4) ___*Physical Body*___ .

It is vitally important that we, as worship ministry members, keep our physical bodies healthy and in-shape. Lack of sleep, bad diet, and an overall lack of physical preparation can hinder your ability to minister. We need to be ready to minister and not be hindered by illness and the like. Vocalists, it is important to warm up your voice so you do not cause long-term damage by abusing your voice. It is even necessary at times for musicians to stretch their hands, arms, etc. so as to not cause long-term damage (carpal-tunnel syndrome or other repetitive-motion injuries, etc.)

II. Discussion

1) What are some of the reasons that you personally do not prepare more for the times of worship?
2) What are some simple ways that we can begin to take steps toward increasing our musical/vocal ability?
3) During a worship service, what are the results of a worship team that has not prepared adequately?
4) How is the congregation affected when there has been a lack of preparation by the ministry team (worship team, pastors, ushers, etc.) as a whole?
5) Why does God anoint preparation? Why can't we just make up for a lack of preparation by praying before the service?

III. Prayer Points

1) Pray that God would give us a fresh revelation of what our role is as a worship team.

2) Pray that God would help us to see how we can re-prioritize our time to help prepare, musically and spiritually, for when we minister (both personally and as a team).

3) Pray that this heart of honoring the Lord through preparation would be on every member of the worship team and ministry team.

4) Pray that we would see an increasing level of the manifest presence of God in our services as we increasingly focus on preparing a place for His presence.

Chapter 9

Platform Protocol

You would think that some things are "obvious" and that common sense would take care of 90% of the necessary guidelines that are required to be in front of people. Not so. The reality is that people need an obvious, consistent, and clearly stated protocol for being on the stage or platform. That protocol should be written and implemented.

In this lesson, we will discuss the guidelines and protocol for platform ministry in the "local church." Due to the subjective nature of this topic, the leadership of every local church needs to customize the protocol for themselves. In this lesson, we will discuss some basic concepts that can be discussed and tailored for your ministry. I would recommend taking some time with your worship team – or at least the core leaders of the team – to discuss, develop, and enforce the particular protocol that will serve your church and worship ministry.

I. The Lesson

Protocol, by definition, is a set of guidelines and boundaries, correct etiquette and procedure. Etiquette and boundaries are necessary and healthy for every worship team. Protocol, policy, rules, standards, expectations and boundaries are not words and concepts that artistic people readily embrace. So it's easy to slip into a very relaxed or subjective application of rules that drain the energy and productivity from the team. When a protocol is established, implemented and enforced it produces consistency, life, and joy in the team.

Many of the guidelines we will discuss are subjective in nature and change from church to church and culture to culture. As we discuss this topic we will attempt to establish a clear understanding of what is desirable, acceptable, and unacceptable when standing before the congregation, or even behind the congregation (sound and media teams). Although this teaching is called "Platform Protocol," we will be discussing these principals as they apply to all those involved in worship ministry. Some will only apply to those in the band or on stage, while some will apply to all.

1) Respect other people's time by being ___*on time*___. This is a huge one for leaders. To make people wait or to be late for an appointment sends the clear message, "Your time is not important to me." Preparation for ministry begins long before we enter the building. So, we must prioritize the set times for rehearsals, sound checks, prayer meetings, and other team meetings. We must do our best to create a culture where we all help each other hold to the standard of punctuality. Have grace with each other but be strong with this standard!

2) Exemplify ___*modesty*___ and temperance (to be moderate and self controlled) by practicing an honest "mirror check" before leaving the house (evaluate your attire in the mirror before you leave). When it comes to dress code, I was raised in Pentecostal legalism (Dave here). So, I understand the unrealistic and even ridiculous expectations that can be put on people in the name of "holiness" or "representing God." Dress codes change from nation to nation, culture to culture and what is appropriate and accepted in Southern California may not be accepted in Washington D.C. We cannot – and should not – attempt to regulate or enforce our standards beyond our local church, but here is what we can all agree on:

> 1 Cor. 10:32-33 *"Do not cause anyone to stumble... Even as I try to please everybody in every way. For I am not seeking my own good but the good of many."*

1 Tim. 4:12 *"Set an example for the believers in speech, in life, in love, in faith and in purity."*

1 Tim. 2:9-10 *"I also want women to dress modestly, with decency and propriety… To dress appropriate for women who profess to worship God."*

A particular dress code and platform protocol needs to be established for every local church. Perhaps a special chat with the ladies from one of the female leaders would be beneficial. Here are three recommendations that we believe would be a good starting point for any worship team:

    a. Don't let your attire – or lack thereof – be a ***distraction*** .
    b. Be free and uniquely you, within the ***boundaries*** and parameters developed by the team.
    c. Develop a culture where it is acceptable and expected to discuss any problems in this area.

3) Don't be trapped by the ***sheet music*** . This is obviously for the musicians and singers. It is quite uninspiring to watch a worship leader who is glued to his/her chord charts and staring at a music stand for 30 minutes. Depending on how many new songs your church learns each month as well as the rotation and consistency of musicians, it may be necessary to have charts available and there is nothing wrong with that. We would just encourage you to "be free" so that you can look at people, lift your eyes to heaven, and express worship without having to concentrate on the next chord or lyric. Don't forget to enjoy yourself too!

4) No chewing ***gum*** !

5) Realize you are always on __*camera*__. Even if your church does not use image magnification with screens and cameras, the concept and ramifications are the same. Try to film your team so you can do a play-back to see what is being communicated. This will help us to be intentional in our behavior without performing.

6) Stay __*connected*__ to the worship leader by keeping your eyes open! This will apply more to the musicians, but should be discussed with everyone as to how well you are staying with the signals that are directing the team. You should also develop solid communication with the media team as to where you are going and what needs to happen next.

7) No __*green room*__ or "drinking fountain retreats!" This is a personal area of concern... well, actually I think the term is "pet peeve" of mine (Dave again). I believe it sends a strong signal to the congregation when the worship team leaves the room after worship. Even if they need to exit through the back of the stage and take a restroom break, I believe the team should be seen finding their seats near the front, Bibles open, ready to hear the Word. Can I get an "amen" on that one?

8) Be ready for the __*ministry time*__. Your church may call it the "altar call". Here's the thought. If you know the pastor is going to call for the musicians at the close of the message, then:
   a. Be seated somewhere close to the front and near an aisle so you can make your way quickly and with minimum distraction to the stage.
   b. Know what song you are going into so you don't have to have a small conference on stage while the pastor is still attempting to communicate to the people. We would recommend the worship leader always have a couple options ready to go. Pull a couple extra chord charts that are appropriate and by the last ten minutes of the message, be thinking about what song would work well.

c. As you go to the platform, try not to move microphone stands, re-string or tune your instrument, or anything else that would not serve the moment.

d. Stay on stage and "flow" until it's an appropriate time to transition from live to CD or DVD (this might be a good point of discussion for your team).

II. Discussion questions

1) How are we doing with showing up on time and respecting other people's time? Are those who have additional set up and preparation requirements making the necessary adjustments?

2) What would be some "platform distractions" that have bothered you as you have watched other teams (be nice and constructive with this one)?

3) How are we doing with "green room worshipers?" Are we setting an example for the church in this area?

4) How are we when it comes to being free from sheet music and able to express ourselves?   What should our expectation be in this area?

5) What specific areas of platform protocol do we need to discuss and implement for our church?

6) How does all that we are discussing here affect the congregation and worship atmosphere, both positively and negatively?

III. Prayer Points

1) Pray for Grace!

2) Pray for maturity in the team and the ability to be challenged by the standards that are being set without becoming offended.

3) Pray for an "excellent spirit" to be over the whole team.

Chapter 10

Plowing in Worship

If you've led worship services or corporate gatherings of the church for any period of time, this title makes *perfect* sense to you. No matter how much prayer, preparation, and thought you've given to the service, sometimes it just feels like you never scratch the surface of the spiritual.

"Lord? Where are you?" you ask. You begin to check your heart and search for sin you haven't repented of. You check with the sound man to make sure the system was actually *on* during the service. What is going on? Has God forsaken you? Has He lifted His hand from your church? Let's assume He hasn't for the sake of this lesson.

This lesson will focus on a necessary component of successful worship services and churches: plowing. There is nothing fun about plowing. It is the dreadfully hard-work portion of agriculture and the less-than-desired reality of worship ministry. We live for the moments in church where the presence of the Lord so fills the room that worship happens naturally. However, God has also called the worship team to "go first" – to take the plow and break the hard ground in the spirit.

It is vitally important to instruct your team in the process of plowing. Not all worship times are going to be an "open-heaven" time where the presence of God is so strong that the congregation has to hide their faces from the public like Moses had to. In fact, it is often necessary to have a faith-filled determination to create an atmosphere where the presence of the Lord is realized. This happens through plowing. Plowing creates freedom in the spirit. Successful plowing takes a worship team that understands its role to break up the hard ground through faith-filled declaration in worship.

If you can get this teaching into the hearts of your team, you will see a tangible difference in your team's approach to worship times. Once you know who the enemy is, it's easy to fight. It is important to relay that information on to the team. The weapons of the enemy are doubt, discouragement, fear, intimidation, and shrinking back in the "heat of battle." Infuse your team with faith. You *must* all take your role as the worshipers and "go first."

We have found that it is the constant teaching and exhortation about plowing that has enabled our team to persevere through hard times in worship. We have had to be sensitive and on the watch for discouragement and doubt in our teams and remind them that our role is to plow the hard ground, whether we see the immediate effects or not. It *will* create an environment that brings forth a great harvest of worshiping hearts and transformed lives.

I. The Lesson

As worship team members, we *live* for the worship services where the presence of God is so tangible that you barely have to do *anything* – God is taking care of the rest. That atmosphere is contagious and addicting.

But what about the times in worship where you feel as if you are as far away from God as you could ever possibly be? The congregation seems to be staring at the stage like deer in headlights. It feels as though the freedom you experienced the week before is a distant memory. In that moment you question your involvement in worship ministry. In that moment it is vitally important to embrace one of the most important roles of the worship team.

> Hosea 10:11-12 *"Judah shall plow... Break up your fallow ground..."*

As a worship team, you must embrace your role in ___*plowing*___ in worship. The word "judah" in the Hebrew is "praise," and so the tribe of Judah is the tribe of the "praisers." Today's application? Judah refers to the worshipers – specifically, the worship team. This verse in Hosea is showing us the important role of the worshipers to break up the fallow ground in the spirit, leading to a "fertile" atmosphere where people can freely meet with God. Let's look at this principle further.

What is the "fallow ground?"
1) Hearts hardened as a result of ___*sin*___, compromise, ___*attitudes*___, past hurts, etc.
2) An unfertile environment of ___*doubt*___ and lack of ___*faith*___ about the truth that God actually *wants* and *desires* to meet with us.
3) Can be the ___*opposition*___ of the enemy to our faith-filled advances as a church.

Purposes of plowing in agriculture[3]:
1) Turning over the soil to bring fresh nutrients to the surface
2) Burying weeds and old crops, allowing them to break down
3) Aerating the soil, allowing it to retain moisture better

Subsequent meaning in the spiritual:
1) ___*Stirring*___ up people's ___*spirits*___ (and thus the spiritual atmosphere) in order to bring the things of the Spirit to the surface.
2) Burying and breaking down the things of the ___*enemy*___, ___*sin*___, and ___*reliance*___ on human strength. All of these elements are blockades that prevent the people of God from meeting with Him freely.

---

[3]   "Plough." *Wikipedia, The Free Encyclopedia*. 20 May 2008, 22:08 UTC. Wikimedia Foundation, Inc. 28 May 2008 <http://en.wikipedia.org/w/index.php?title=Plough&oldid=213806399>.

3) Tenderizing hearts, allowing them to receive the things of the Spirit of God easier (eg. revelation of God in worship, the preaching of the Word, etc.).

As we can see, plowing in worship is a faith-filled determination that *doesn't back down when hard ground is discovered.* Hard ground is simply an indication that its time to get out the "plow" as a worship team. In Biblical times (and throughout history across all civilizations), the vitality and existence of entire people groups was dependent upon someone who understood how to plow when they encountered hard, fallow ground. If when every time hard ground was discovered the farmers gave up and quit, an entire people group would die of starvation.

Get the picture? An entire group of people – men and women of God, desperate for the "food" of His presence – are depending on us as a worship team to not shrink back when hard ground is discovered. If we do shrink back, they die spiritually and as a church. Instead, they are relying on us to take up the "plow" and do what we know to do: praise God, declare His Name and His renown among His people, play and sing in faith and determination, and believe God for breakthrough for His people. We are the praisers (Judah). "Judah shall plow."

II. Discussion

1) When was a time recently when you felt like we, as the worship team, were "plowing"?

2) What can you do as a musician/singer to do *your* part in "plowing"?

3) What are the results (spiritually and naturally) of a worship team that does not "plow" when a worship time is hard/rough?

4) What are the results (spiritually and naturally) of a worship team that *does* "plow" when a worship time is hard/rough?

III. Prayer Points

1) Pray that God would infuse us with a new level of faith as a worship team.
2) Pray that God would break the bondages of sin, compromise, attitudes, and past hurts off of His people so they can experience freedom in worship.
3) Pray for your worship time this coming weekend, that it would be a time of freedom and liberty in the presence of the Lord! Make this a continual prayer focus in your personal times and as a worship team.

Chapter 11

Production Elements in Worship

⟋⟍⟋⟍

One of the most frustrating things about being a worship overseer is to put all the time and effort into preparation and execution of the worship time, only to find out that the sound was so horrible, that it was actually *hindering* people from meeting with God. If you're like me, you've asked for feedback after a service and heard the response, "I couldn't really hear your voice at all." How frustrating!

This isn't a lesson on how to find a good sound engineer (although good sound is *definitely* dependent on one). It is about how you – as the worship overseer – and your band can begin to set your sound personnel up for success by looking at how you approach the production/orchestration of what happens on stage.

For example, if your drummer cannot play consistently "in time," there's nothing the sound person can do to make the drums "in time." If the pitch of your voice is consistently flat, the sound person cannot make your voice in pitch *for* you (without spending the money Ozzie does – sorry Ozzie).

The basis for this discussion is, "What are we giving the sound engineer to work with? How are we contributing to a good mix by our production/orchestration on stage?" In this brief lesson, you will not be able to cover *everything* there is to know about production, but the goal should be to get your team to begin thinking differently about what they play/sing. How are they contributing to a worshipful, distraction-free atmosphere? Are they working to blend and work in harmony with the other instruments/singers on the team?

If you can get your team to begin to focus on these concepts more and more, you will notice a *drastic* difference in how the worship times come across to the congregation. Your sound engineer(s) will be forever grateful for your efforts and will be empowered to do what they do well. I believe you will begin to see a difference *immediately* and it will in turn give your team a new "wind in their sails" as they begin to hear feedback from the congregation and sound engineer of things like, "Man, you sound *great* today!"

NOTE: One of the best ways to start focusing on this is to pick a song in your rehearsal time and go through the production elements listed in this lesson one-by-one until the entire team can tell the difference between what good and bad production sounds like. You may even want to have them all demonstrate the extremes. For example, "Everyone play as LOUD and as MUCH as you can." Then after you do that, "Now, let's pay attention to dynamics and make each section have a *noticeable* change in dynamics from the previous one."

*This lesson could conceivably be a two-part lesson that you cover over two weeks.

I. The Lesson

Have you ever experienced the following situation? You received a new song from the worship leader at rehearsal that really excited you, and so you were motivated to put in *extra* time to figure out parts/fills/vocal lines that you think would work *wonderfully*. At service, you executed your parts flawlessly only to find out later that people couldn't hear you at all! What rises up in your heart after something like this? Frustration? A desire to kill the sound man?

Have you ever considered the possibility that maybe the problem from the beginning was in fact… you? In the world of music production (recording), great records happen when much time and consideration is given to the production of the songs.

Production = the __*musical elements*__ and __*crafting*__ of a song

Production Elements:

        Dynamics : the perceived volume of parts and sections of a song (ranging from quiet to loud)

        Rhythm /Groove: the rhythmic structure of the song/ "feel" of how the rhythm works within the music (usually determined by the drums)

        Arrangement : the organization within each song of when each instrument plays/doesn't play, and how the instruments/voices work together

        Timbre : the sound each instrument/vocalist makes (eg. guitar tone, keyboard sounds, drum tuning/selection, etc.)

There are other production elements as well, but these are the main ones to consider. In the world of music production, it is when the production elements of a song are considered with great scrutiny that the overall "mix" of the music sounds better. The basic premise for this is the familiar saying, "Garbage in, garbage out." Let's bring further clarification.

If a guitar is out of tune on stage, there is nothing the sound engineer can do to fix it using the sound board (other than turning it off!). If the drummer is not playing consistent "time," there is nothing the sound engineer can do to make him play *in* time. If every person on the stage is playing/singing as *loud* and as *much* as they can for the *entire* song, the mix in the congregation will be very chaotic and messy.

So, our goal as a worship team is to begin to focus on these production elements so that we empower the sound engineer to be able to mix to the best of his/her ability. How can we work together to minimize musical distractions and create the best opportunity for people to meet with God? A good mix helps people meet with God. Good production in the worship team helps achieve a good mix.

Items to focus on in regard to production:

1) ___Listen___ to each other. In order to "gel" well with the team, you have to be *listening* to what each person on the team is playing/singing. In times of spontaneous/prophetic worship, it is important to see what is being sung/played that may be what God is breathing on in that moment.
    a. Bass players: What is the groove the drummer is playing? What is the left hand of the piano player doing?
    b. Electric guitarists: What is the piano playing? What is the acoustic playing? What are the singers singing
    c. Acoustic players: What is the piano playing? What are the singers singing?
    d. Singers: What is the worship leader singing/doing. Is he/she backing off of his/her microphone to let the congregation sing? You do the same

2) ___Leave room___ for each other. If everyone is playing the same thing at the same time, it usually "clutters" or "muddies" the mix. If there is a featured vocal line, piano part, or lead solo, it is important that the rest of the instruments/vocalists play or sing less to create more "room" in the music and in the mix for that part to be heard. If the arrangement doesn't allow for this "room," the featured part will not translate well in the mix. In a spontaneous/prophetic moment, if the prophetic vocal or instrument cannot be heard, we have hindered its effectiveness in the congregation.
    Examples:
    a. Acoustic guitar can play only the higher strings to leave room for the bass and piano to carry the lower parts
    b. Electric guitar should be careful not to play in the same octaves as the vocals are singing so the words and melodies of the vocalists (especially the lead vocalist) can be heard easily by the congregation

   c. Drummer should simplify drum/groove patterns to allow other instruments (eg. acoustic guitar) to carry the rhythm at certain moments.

   d. Vocalists should refrain from singing if one of the vocalists begins to sing a spontaneous/prophetic song until a repetitive hook or line is being sung. At that point, singing with that person helps to reinforce that thought/declaration.

3) Think in ___*gears*___.[4] If you think of the arrangement and intensity of a song in terms of gears (like in that of a car), you want to make sure that you don't get to the highest gear too early. In order to emphasize anthemic, key moments of songs, you have to save the highest gears for that moment.

For example, in the song "How Great is Our God" by Chris Tomlin, the sixth gear should be saved for the bridge, when the congregation sings, "Name above all names..." If the band is in sixth gear at the chorus, it doesn't leave any room to build into the bridge and make it sound any different from the chorus. An example of how to think of the production of "How Great is Our God" in terms of gears would be the following:

Section	Gear	Production Example
Verse 1	1st gear	Acoustic only with lead vocal
Chorus 1	2nd gear	Acoustic and piano, vocals
Verse 2	3rd gear	Bass, drums, electric (gently)
Chorus 2	4th gear	Intensity builds, not 100% yet
Bridge	6th gear	Powerful! Anthemic!
Chorus 3	4th gear	Drums and vocals only
Chorus 4	5th gear	Band back in for final time

---

[4]   Thanks to Brent Milligan

II. Discussion

1) What are the production elements that we as a team are doing well right now?
2) What are the production elements that we need to work on as a team?
3) Who in our congregation can help to keep us accountable in regard to paying attention to production elements? (hint: these people should be unbiased and have a musical "ear")
4) What are the spiritual results of a band who pays careful attention to the production elements listed in this lesson?
5) What can we do as a band (as a group and individually) to grow in our awareness and execution of production elements in worship?

III. Prayer Points

1) God delights in excellence. Pray that God would increase our spirit of excellence as we worship – week in, week out.
2) Pray that God would make us sensitive to and aware of His leading and that we would be able to musically facilitate the move of the Spirit more effectively.
3) Pray over the atmosphere of your worship services, that distractions of any kind would be minimized and that the services would be a place for people to meet with God easily.
4) Pray that the Lord would unify the team to a greater measure. It is then that we are better able to flow together, both musically and spiritually.

Chapter 12

Rehearsal Protocol

Rehearsal can be one of the most profitable times as well as one of the most frustrating wastes of time. If you've been leading worship or overseeing a worship ministry for any period of time, I'm sure you have experienced both sides of the spectrum. Although your preparation as a leader has *much* to do with the success or failure of a rehearsal, this lesson will help you address the aspects that are up to each band member.

What good is it to prepare the set list, have the chord charts ready to pass out, arrive a half hour early, and make sure the sound is operating correctly if no one in the band shows up for rehearsal? Have you ever experienced a time when you were unsure about the direction of a song and the band attacked the song like a pack of ravenous wolves? Have you had a band filled with musicians who feel the need to practice every "chop" they have at the same time, all while you are trying to give direction?

Rehearsal protocol or etiquette is vital to the success of your rehearsals as well as to your sanity as a leader. As you go through this lesson (and discussion), continue to reinforce in your team that the end goal is for rehearsals that run smoothly, effectively prepare the team for the worship time, and are completed in a timely manner. If this result remains the goal, there will be grace to bring correction (even forcefully at times). Your heart isn't to be a power-hungry, dictatorial worship leader but to serve the team by honoring their time and commitment.

As you implement the protocol laid out in this lesson (or a version of it), we encourage you to review these elements with your team before you begin rehearsal for the next several occasions until they "get it." In our experience, the small rebuke is more than compensated for by the fact that rehearsals end earlier and that they set the team up for success during the worship service.

I. The Lesson

This lesson is a little different than some of the other lessons in this series. We're not going to dig into deep spiritual principles or exegete scripture. Rather, we're going to look at several elements that go into making rehearsal times more timely and productive. Let's call it "rehearsal protocol."

There is nothing more frustrating than making time in your busy schedule to come to worship rehearsal and then ending up wasting time, feeling unproductive, or staying *way* past the normal time. The tendency is to blame these types of rehearsals on the worship leader. And while you are correct in thinking that the worship leader has a lot to do with the productivity and timeliness of rehearsals, so does the worship team, as well. We'll deal with the worship leaders later. For now, let's look at several elements that you, as the worship team, can put into practice in order for rehearsals to be productive and timely.

1) If you're ___*on time*___, you're __*late*__!
     - What time does rehearsal begin? Figure out how long it takes you to set up your instrument, monitor, or warm up your voice. Work backward from the time rehearsal begins to allow for this preparation and plan on arriving then.

     Example: If rehearsal begins at 7:00pm and it takes you 20 minutes to setup your amp, dial in your tone, and tune up, then you should arrive to rehearsal at 6:40pm.

- One of the most frustrating things for the worship leader and the rest of the worship team is when one or more of the members are late – it delays *everything*!

2) Come __*prepared*__ .

- Make sure your gear works, you have sufficient cables, your strings are fresh (and you have all your strings), or you have an ample supply of drumsticks. Even coming to rehearsal early doesn't do any good when you don't have what you need to be successful. Take ownership of your instrument/craft and be prepared! Check your gear in enough time to do something about it if it is not adequate for rehearsal.

3) Come to rehearsal __*happy*__ .

- A grumpy, angry, discouraged, or otherwise unpleasant attitude stands *directly* in the way of team unity (see "One Accord" and "Byproducts of Unity"). If you are really going through something, ask the other team members and your worship leader to pray for you. Transparency and honesty are powerful "unity builders" in the team.

4) Don't create __*musical chaos*__ !

- Don't feel the need to practice every fill, lick, run, part, vocal line, etc. that you've ever thought of playing. This should be saved for your personal practice times (you *are* practicing, right?).

- It is immensely frustrating for the team and worship leader when the musicians play when a specific part is being worked on with one or a group of the members of the team.

- Even if you are working on a specific part for the song being rehearsed, be sensitive and make sure that you're doing that at the right time. Practicing the right part and the wrong time contributes to musical chaos.

5) Take adequate __*notes*__ !

> - Never come to rehearsal without a pen/pencil. Why spend an hour or two rehearsing only to leave and forget every production element that was worked on during the rehearsal? This is not only frustrating to the worship leader and team, but hinders the worship "flow" and creates more work for you in the long-run.
>
> - Additionally, make sure you then *take your chord charts/notes home* in order to practice and then *bring them with you to the worship service.*
>
> - There is nothing more reassuring to a worship leader than to see members of the team with a pen in their hands, taking notes.

6) Be ready to __*contribute*__ and __*submit*__ .

> - If you can offer help to another member on the team with his/her part, be ready to offer it in humility. If you withhold your knowledge of the part/song, the team suffers.
>
> - If your idea or part is determined to be inappropriate for the song (for whatever reason), be ready and willing to submit to the leader. Willing submission to leadership brings the blessing of God on the team. Defiant opposition brings disunity and all the negative byproducts thereof (see "Byproducts of Unity).

7) Don't become annoyed when the leader brings extra elements to the rehearsal.

> - Examples are: these lessons, prayer times, watching a DVD, etc. Understand that these additional elements are designed to build up the team as a whole. Even if you've got it all figured out (first off, you probably need to pay *special* attention if you think you have), understand that other members of the team are benefiting from it, even if you are not.

II. Discussion

1) What are the results of unproductive and untimely rehearsals?
2) What are the results of productive and timely rehearsals due to musicians following "rehearsal protocol?"
3) How can we, as a team, lovingly encourage each other to follow these guidelines week-by-week? (Doing it in a wrong way creates tension and spite between team-members.)
4) What are the effects of productive rehearsals on the congregation?

III. Prayer Points

1) Pray? About rehearsing? We're not going to tell you to "Pray that your drummer buys drumsticks"
2) This week, you're on your own. Take prayer requests from the team.

Chapter 13

Spiritual Unity in the Worship Team – Pt. 1

~~~⦿~~~

Unity is one of the most important topics when discussing worship or any other form of team ministry. Any time people are gathered together for the sake of a particular ministry, it is vitally important that they are in unity – one focus, one heart, one mind, one goal.

Let's be honest, though. No matter how good this looks on paper, achieving unity in reality is quite an elusive task at times. One person may come in so physically sick that he/she is just trying to get through the service(s) to the best of his/her ability; another may have a slight personality conflict with someone else on the team; another on the team may be so worried about executing his/her part correctly they ignore the other members on the team.

These situations, and more, can be seen in teams all over the world. In our experience, there are many local-church worship teams who go through weekend after weekend and are plagued by politics, personal conflict, immature actions, etc. These teams then wonder why their worship experiences are a roller-coaster of good and bad days and why they feel like they're not "getting anywhere."

As a leader, it is important that you not only work to cultivate and protect team unity, but also make it a serious matter of prayer. If your team is not unified – in any way – it will be impossible to reach your full potential and "hit the mark" as a worship team. The common misconception is that, as the leader, you'll be able to "carry" the team if you have to. But when you dig into the Biblical principles discussed in the next two lessons, you'll see how important it is to guard unity at all costs.

In this lesson, we discuss the idea of being in "one accord." Not being in one accord has certain negative effects, but being in one accord has great benefits to the church as a whole.

I. The Lesson

> "Can two people walk together without agreeing on the direction?"
> Amos 3:3

This concept of agreement/unity applies to much more than just worship ministry. But for our discussion, we'll obviously be focusing on the concept of being in agreement or spiritual unity within the worship team. How can we minister to the Lord and lead the congregation into His presence if we are not in unity?

You may have seen (and possibly created) these situations before:

- John and Susan used to be romantically involved and the entire team knows that any time they're on the team together there is tension.
- Fred is new to the team and relatively new to the church. His worship theology varies from that of the church.
- Martha is a background vocalist, but she really wants to sing the lead on the songs. This is a common area of contention for her and is a common roadblock to her effectiveness.
- Bill the bass player just heard an unsubstantiated claim against the youth pastor that Bill hasn't dealt with properly. This has affected his 100% trust of the leadership, even though the claim was completely false.

All of the above situations are examples of instances in worship ministry that can cause unity to be thwarted.

The phrase "one accord" is used 12 times in the Bible, 11 of which are in the book of Acts. The common thread of "one accord" throughout this book must not be ignored.

Of the 11 times "one accord" is used in Acts, seven times were in the context of the outpouring of the Holy Spirit, miracles being released, and the Body of Christ being strengthened. The other four times were detailed instances of a crowd rising up against the apostles. In both sets of cases, being in one accord preceded a release of **_power_** (whether good or bad). When we as a worship ministry are in one accord, it leads to a release of power in the Lord.

One accord = with one ___*mind*___ , with one ___*passion*___ .

> Being in one accord leads to the release of the power of the Holy Spirit, the strengthening of the Church, and makes the way for salvation for the lost.

As a worship team, we MUST operate in one accord, not for the sake of saying we're a great team, but so that we position ourselves to be used by God in a mighty way. He wants to touch His people, and He has purposed in His heart to use us to do it. So, let's be in unity for the sake of His people.

II. Discussion

1) What are some of the obstacles to achieving unity in our team?
2) What are the ramifications of politics on team unity?
3) How can we as a team work to be in "one accord"?
4) What can the release of power look like in our worship times when we are in "one accord"?

III. Prayer Points

1) Pray that our worship team(s) would be united each time they step on the platform.
2) Pray that barriers to unity would be destroyed (i.e. selfishness, personal conflict, etc.).

3) Pray for a sense of "one accord" on the congregation.
4) Pray that there would be a release of power in the church as a result of the unity of the worship team.

Chapter 14

Spiritual Unity in the Worship Team – Pt. 2

In part one of the series on spiritual unity, we looked at the power of being in one accord. In this lesson, we will be looking at further byproducts of unity. There are certain intangible benefits that come with unity that are essential for the gatherings of the Church to be as God designed them to be.

It is important, as a leader, that you instruct your team in unity, guard unity, pray for unity – basically, do anything you can to cultivate unity in your worship team. We'll be looking at Psalm 133 in this lesson and at the concept of the "commanded blessing" of the Lord. The key to unlocking the reward of the "commanded blessing" is to be in unity.

Through implementing strategies to create and protect unity in our teams, we have seen the byproducts of unity in our congregation. The concepts you're about to deliver seem a bit ethereal at times, but as you teach, pray, and implement strategies to create and maintain unity in your team, you too will begin to see an amazing shift in the spiritual atmosphere of your church.

We urge you to ask the tough questions, have the tough chats with people on your team. Whatever it takes to maintain unity is worth the effort. Any hindrance to the unity of your team results in the withholding of the commanded blessing of the Lord on your team and congregation.

I. The Lesson

In the last lesson, we learned about the power that is released when we are in one accord as a team. It was demonstrated extensively in the book of Acts that being in one accord leads to a release of the power of the Holy Spirit. Additionally, being unified (in one accord) leads to the Body of Christ being strengthened and leads to the salvation of the lost.

In this lesson, we'll be looking at another instance in the Bible where unity is given emphasis.

> Psalm 133 *"Behold, how good and how pleasant it is for brethren to dwell together in unity! ²It is like the precious oil upon the head, running down on the beard, the beard of Aaron, running down on the edge of his garments. ³It is like the dew of Hermon, descending upon the mountains of Zion; for there the LORD commanded the blessing – life forevermore."*

Psalm 133 paints a pretty vivid picture of the byproducts of unity. King David had a revelation of the goodness and the pleasantness that comes with being in unity. He had seen them first-hand – the byproducts of unity.

"It is like precious oil"

The oil David was speaking of here was the oil that Aaron would have been anointed with. The anointing oil was made up of four very aromatic spices that could be smelled from a far way off. When someone was being anointed, everyone knew it.

Unity, like anointing, ___***affects***___ more than just those who are in unity.

The congregation can "smell" when there is or isn't unity among the worship team (and leadership team).

No unity = no___*fragrance*___ (blessing, favor, freedom in worship)

"It is like the dew of Hermon"

The context of the scripture here provides a very vivid picture of what David was talking about. Cool air coming from the Mediterranean Sea ascends up the side of Mount Hermon creating a cool dew that "descends on the mountains of Zion."

The dew in Jerusalem (Zion) was cool, ___*refreshing*___, and life-giving. Unity has this effect on the Church.

The "dew of Hermon" was a symbol of the blessing of God on Jerusalem. So, too, does unity lead to the ___*blessing*___ of God on our churches and in our worship times.

"For there the Lord commanded the blessing"

As previously stated, ___*blessing*___ is one of the most incredible byproducts of unity. But this kind of blessing isn't just a glib, "I hope we get blessed" kind of blessing. It is the ___*commanded*___ blessing of the Lord.

Commanded = to ___*charge*___, give orders

So, when God commands a blessing, blessing – like a soldier – has no choice but to "obey" and be dispatched to the ones whom God is blessing. So, make no mistake about it: When God commands a blessing, *there will be blessing!*

"Life Forevermore"

There are many possibilities for what the "blessing of the Lord" could be. By this scripture, however, we are told that it is "life forevermore." What an awesome inheritance of the unified ones... LIFE FOREVERMORE!

Worship services that function as God intended produce **_everlasting life_** for those who partake! Who wouldn't want to go to *that* church? There are too many churches where no life exists in the Spirit. This is not how the Lord intended our churches to be. Churches, worship teams, and congregations that are unified are targets for the true life of the Holy Spirit. This atmosphere is irresistible to the lost, the broken, the hurting, the oppressed and the lonely. Unity is the key to unlocking the commanded blessing of the Lord – life forevermore.

II. Discussion

1) If unity is a pleasing "scent" to the church, what would produce a scent that is unpleasing?
2) Practically, how does the congregation experience the byproducts of unity in a worship service?
3) What happens in/to a church when there is no unity in the leadership/worship team?
4) What happens in a church when unity is protected and maintained, week in and week out?

III. Prayer Points

1) Pray that every barrier to unity would be torn down in our worship team.
2) Pray that God would help our team to be unified week in and week out.
3) Pray that we, as the worship team, would be a channel of life to our congregation.

Chapter 15

Stewardship of our Gifts

As pastors, teachers, and ministry leaders, part of our responsibility is to teach those we are leading how to effectively "steward" their gifts and talents with wisdom, balance, and passion so that our team can be used for the great purposes of God. The challenge is to stretch people and bring them up to a biblical standard of service and sacrifice without their getting bent, bitter, or burnt in the process.

In calling people to the high-call of using their gifts and talents for God, there is always a continuum of responses and personality types that need to be addressed and corrected. On one side of the continuum, there is the zealous, super-spiritual, hyper-prophetic visionary who wants to quit their job and just worship God 24/7. On the other side of the continuum, there is the lethargic, irresponsible, melancholic, dreamer who has great potential and gifting but hasn't figured out how to set an alarm clock.

Your job as the leader is to establish a biblical standard of prioritization and stewardship that can be modeled and reproduced. So, the need to teach strong commitment and sacrifice must be balanced with the principles of "Sabbath rest" and a "yoke" that is easy! Our goal in this lesson is to help the team understand the privilege and responsibility of stewardship and how this is a vital component in the development of their gifts and talents.

As you present this topic to your team, be sure to open up some discussion regarding what they feel they have been given and how they will personally give an account to God for their gifts as they stand before Christ on "the big day."

I. The Lesson

Matthew 25:14-29 is the parable where Jesus discussed the reality of stewardship and being entrusted with talents. A real moment of revelation and maturation occurs when we realize that our gifts and talents – whether musical, technical, artistic, communication, or resources – are not ours to determine how we are or are not going to use them. All of us have been entrusted with a level of gifting and talent that requires stewardship and responsibility.

An accurate way to view the talents and abilities that you have been given is to **see yourself as a manager and not an owner**. This will bring an accurate perspective and help develop consistency in serving. In managing what God, "The Master," has given us, there are principles and potential traps that we need to be aware of and/or deal with.

1) God has given us the talents and gifts that we posses because he expects us to __*invest*__ them in His kingdom.

Matt. 25:27 *"'Well then, you should have put my money on deposit with the bankers, so that when I returned I would have received it back with interest.'"*

A common error is to assume that we can use or not use our talents based on our level of interest, passion, and sense of fulfillment. It's that attitude of, "Yeah, I can sing. But I'm just really not into it." This is the wrong way to view your God-given abilities. For someone with an incredible voice, teaching gift, ability to create graphic art, or someone highly gifted in sound engineering to not invest those gifts for the cause of Christ is to **position themselves as the owner instead of the manager.**

2) The lack of investment (consistent usage for the Master's work) will not only cause our talents and gifts to lie dormant, but will actually result in the diminishing or **removal** of the gifts. What happens when an athlete quits working out for a year or two? What about someone learning a foreign language that makes progress and then quits for a couple years? You don't just go back to the place you were when you stopped! Can you think of someone you know who has experienced this principle?

> Matt. 25:28 "'Take the talent from him and give it to the one who has the ten talents.'"

3) There will always be someone who has "more talents" and a higher level of gifting than you do! A consistent and predictable trap for musicians, singers, and those in performing arts is to compare our talents and gifts with those around us. This results in either the sin of **pride** or the debilitating effects of **discouragement**. (more on this in the lesson "The Snare of Comparison")

> Matt. 25:15 "To one he gave five talents of money, to another two talents, and to another one talent, each according to his ability. Then he went on his journey."

4) Good stewards have **discovered** what their talents are and have committed to the process of **developing** those talents. This process of development is very practical, even predictable, and in the arena of worship ministry includes:

a. Weekly rehearsals
b. Private lessons and practice time
c. Attending conferences and seminars
d. Submitting to those who lead the worship ministry
e. Punctuality and consistency
f. A high level of local church commitment/ involvement
g. Being faithful in the "small things"
h. Serving wherever needed
i. Listening and viewing new music
j. Staying current with gear and technical advancements
k. Finding mentors and instructors to learn from

1 Cor. 4:2 *"Moreover (firstly, above all other requirements) it is required in stewards that one be found faithful."*

5) **Stewardship** _connects_ **and affects all of life!** One area of mismanagement of our time, talent, and treasure has huge impact on other areas, even if they are seemingly disconnected. The way we manage our bodies through discipline or neglect has a direct impact on our gifts and talents. For example: If I stay up Saturday night playing video games until 3:00 a.m. when I have to sing tenor at the 8:30a.m. Service, then… get the picture?

6) Desire, personal fulfillment, and/or fun are not the highest and most accurate motivations in developing our gifts and talents for God. Ultimately, we will stand before Him and give _an account_ . This is a sobering reality as well as an awesome privilege and responsibility.

Luke 12:48 "To whom much is given, from him much will be required."

II. Discussion

1) How can we be good stewards of our time, talent, and resources without getting burnt-out or out of balance with life and ministry?
2) What could responsible stewardship look like for worship team members of a local church, our church?
3) What are some practical and effective ways to discover your gifts and talents?
4) What is the greatest test for a "one-talent" person?
5) How could we see a greater return on what God has invested in our team? Is poor stewardship in any area limiting our potential?
6) How can poor stewardship in the areas of our time, diet, exercise or entertainment directly affect the return on other gifts and talents? (What would be some common abuses?)
7) What will you personally have to stand before God and answer for in regards to the talents and gifts that you have been given? How would you do if today was that day? *(perhaps a couple brave people could give a response)*

III. Prayer Points

1) Pray that everyone on the team, and those who will be added, will live with a revelation that we are mangers and not owners of our gifts and talents.
2) Pray for a spirit of wisdom and revelation regarding how to invest what we have been given in order to see the greatest return for our church and for eternity.
3) Pray for protection from comparison and repent of any jealousy, discouragement, or pride that might be present as a result of differing levels of talent.
4) Pray for a greater revelation that the "Owner" is coming back for a return on His investment!

Chapter 16

The Anointing

The purpose of this lesson is to bring a greater awareness and increased desire for the work of the Holy Spirit upon and through our worship ministries. The "anointing" can be described and defined several ways, so for the sake of this teaching let's define anointing as: ***The power and presence of the Holy Spirit that is poured upon those who are called to do the works of Christ***.

In the Old Testament, the anointing oil was a precious and sacred formula that was reserved for those who ministered in the house of the Lord. One of the primary prerequisites for serving in the temple was to be "consecrated by the anointing." This was the literal process of having oil poured over the body and garments of the priest (see Exodus 30:20-32).

We have all been in worship services where the music was being played, the lights were working, the people were in the room, and the "machinery" was running but there was an obvious absence of "oil." The absence of the anointing will turn a potentially powerful worship gathering into a "grinding," dead routine.

The anointing is not an emotional or sensory measurement where we ask each other, "How did you feel?" but rather a very objective reality and work of the Holy Spirit that is released in our gatherings. Although we cannot determine the level or work of the Holy Spirit, we can prepare our teams in faith to be anointed vessels in the house of the Lord.

I. The Lesson

"The anointing" can be one of those subjective biblical phrases that can mean different things to different people based upon our understanding and interpretation. It is, in fact, a Biblical concept and requirement, both Old and New Testament. It is important that we understand what the anointing is, why we need it, and how to receive and carry it. How would you define anointing? When someone says, "That was an anointed worship set," or, "She was anointed," or, "He is an anointed singer," what are they saying? (go ahead, chat it up)

> 1) The Old Testament definition of the anointing: The special oil that was prescribed and required by God to be applied to the priests in order to set them apart for ministry in the house of the Lord.
>
> > Exodus 40:13-15 *"Then dress Aaron in the sacred garments, anoint him and consecrate him so he may serve me as priest. Bring his sons and dress them in tunics. Anoint them just as you anointed their father, so they may serve me as priests. Their anointing will be to a priesthood that will continue for all generations to come."*
> >
> > Because this was a prerequisite and a mandatory requirement for all priests who ministered before the Lord, it would be accurate to say: "Where there is no anointing, there is no ___*true ministry*___ !"
>
> 2) One of the New Testament / Greek words for anointing is *"Chraomai,"* which means, "To furnish or give what it is needed. To light upon or rest upon.
> Another word that is used is *"Chrio,"* which means, "To be set apart for service, the divine enabling for the office."
>
> > 2 Cor. 1:21 *"Now it is God who makes both us and you stand firm in Christ. He anointed us. (chrio)"*

So when someone says, "They are anointed," they would be accurately describing someone who the Holy Spirit has rested upon to __*enable them*__ to do what they are called to do. The anointing makes things unique, special, beyond human capabilities, and set apart for God's purpose. The anointing qualifies us to be "priests" in the presence of God and to minister to the Lord and His people. The anointing is always given for a __*purpose*__ .

> Luke 4:18 *"The Spirit of the Lord is on me, because he has anointed me to preach good news to the poor. He has sent me to proclaim freedom for the prisoners and recovery of sight for the blind, to release the oppressed"*

> Acts 1:8 *"But you shall receive power, ability, efficiency and might when the Holy Spirit has come upon you. And you shall be..."*

> Luke 3:22 *"Now when all the people were baptized, and when Jesus also had been baptized, and (while He was still) praying, the (visible) heaven was opened, and the Holy Spirit descended upon Him in bodily form, like a dove."*

3) We need the anointing because human talent, passion, and gifting will not produce __*spiritual results*__ .

> Isaiah 10:27 "In that day their burden will be lifted from your shoulders, their yoke from your neck. The yoke will be destroyed because of the anointing."

> Spiritual yokes (bondages, restraints, and restrictions) are broken and destroyed by the anointing upon the people of God.

4) We need continual anointing because without "fresh oil" we will inevitably face __*burn out*__ and spiritual exhaustion.

There is a clear picture of this in Leviticus chapter 24, when God told the priest that, "The lamps on the pure gold lamp stand before the LORD must be tended continually."

These golden lamp stands were designed to burn fresh oil that would be drawn up from a basin that was being replenished every day. There is a huge difference between being a lamp stand and a candle! Candles consume themselves in the process of providing light while lamp stands are a channel for fresh oil and can burn continually without exhaustion. Ministries that are running on talent, passion, human wisdom, schedules, and budgets without being replenished with the "fresh oil" of the Holy Spirit are candle ministries that have a predictable shelf life!

5) How do we receive and maintain the anointing?

There are several biblical principles and practices that determine the release and levels of anointing that people experience and operate in. The final point is this: The anointing is given to the vessels that are ___*set apart*___ for service in the courts of the Lord!

Exodus 30:29-31 *"You shall consecrate them so they will be most holy, and whatever touches them will be holy. Anoint Aaron and his sons and consecrate them so they may serve me as priests. Say to the Israelites, 'This is to be my sacred anointing oil for the generations to come.'"*

When we are "consecrated," it means that we are set apart *from* something in order to be set apart *to* something. This is the call that has been given to worship leaders, worship teams, musicians, singers, artists, and servants since the establishing of the priesthood. The clear call is to live "holy unto the Lord." This is not a legalistic set of rules but a lifestyle of holiness, purity, integrity, worship, and prayer that makes us different, unique, and usable for the Master.

2 Tim. 2:20-21 *"In a large house there are articles not only of gold and silver, but also of wood and clay; some are for noble purposes and some for ignoble. If a man cleanses himself from the latter, he will be **an instrument for noble purposes**, made holy, useful to the Master and prepared to do any good work."*

II. Discussion

1) When was the first time that you felt the anointing? What did that produce in your heart and desires?
2) Do we value the anointing? How is it a priority for us personally and our team?
3) How can you tell the difference between performance-based and anointed worship?
4) What are some biblical ways that we can receive and walk in the anointing?
5) Why do we need anointing?   How does it affect the congregation?
6) What are some things that will cause the anointing to "leak out"?

III. Prayer Points

1) Pray for a strong desire for the Presence of the Holy Spirit on every aspect of the team: Musically, technically, leadership, etc.
2) Ask for "divine enablement" for your specific area of ministry.
3) Pray for unity (Psalm 133) and that nothing would steal or diminish the anointing.
4) Believe for such a strong anointing on the coming days of worship that the bondages in people's lives would be broken and permanently destroyed during the worship set.
5) Pray for, look for, and anticipate the gifts of the Spirit being in operation as well as a tangible increase in the anointing.
6) Pray for holiness, purity, and integrity to permeate the team! That we would live as "vessels of honor."
7) "MORE LORD!"

Chapter 17

The Language of Worship

We are always looking, searching, striving, and investing to create *good sound*! And just about the time you think you've got a "good mix," something changes. Yet week after week, we continue to search for that ever elusive "perfect mix."

In this lesson we want to talk about the "other sound" that the worship team is responsible for. It is not just the sound of melodies and harmonies, decibels and rhythms, but the sounds that are heard loud and clear in the spirit realm – the sounds of unity or the opposite: division.

There is a language that we must teach our teams and then review over and over. It is the the language of faith, edification, thankfulness, and unity. It is a difficult language to master and it's easy to forget. Therefore, it takes practice, consistent usage, and accountability to become proficient in it.

In this lesson, we will discuss the power of our tongues and the ability to destroy with our conversations the things that we work so hard to produce with our worship. The goal is to bring awareness and accountability to the team when it comes to this area of speaking life or death.

I. The Lesson

Col. 4:6 *"Let your conversation be always full of grace"*

The worship level in a church or community is determined by far more than the worship experience that happens while the band is playing during the services. It's been accurately said, "What takes us years to build with our talent can be destroyed overnight by our character;" and, what takes time and effort to build with our worship team efforts can be destroyed by the power of the tongue.

The sound of worship is not necessarily a song or a band cranking out the latest tunes. Worship is a sound that brings pleasure to the heart of God! This means that our worship-life happens more off the stage than on, more in the secret place than when the lights are shining bright.

Our instruments, our words, our talents, and our influence with people can bring great blessing to the heart of God and His people or they can bring great destruction. Lucifer is the first and most obvious example of what a being that was created for worship can become when his gifts and abilities turn away from the purpose of God. "Those who create the most beautiful sounds carry great potential to release the most destructive sounds."

Another example is Miriam. She was a worship leader and a person of influence that was used by God. However, she allowed the language of faith to be replaced with the language of criticism and division.

> Exo. 15:20-21 *"Then Miriam the prophetess, Aaron's sister, took a tambourine in her hand, and all the women followed her, with tambourines and dancing. Miriam sang to them: "Sing to the LORD, for he is highly exalted."*

Miriam was recorded in the Bible as being a co-leader of one of the most powerful and influential worship services in the history of Israel. Consider it, nearly three million people all rejoicing and celebrating their freedom from the bondage of Egypt that had enslaved their people for generations! Miriam picks up a tambourine and all the ladies begin to dance as she sings to them. Her voice and leadership gift had great influence.

But we soon find her being used by the enemy to bring accusation against God's leader, bring division among the people, and cause the progress of an entire nation to be halted in the middle of a desert! Please read Numbers 12 in its entirety to understand how God responds when people speak out criticism and divisive things. It's quite scary!

> Num. 12:1-4 *"Miriam and Aaron began to talk against Moses because of his Cushite wife, for he had married a Cushite. [2]'Has the LORD spoken only through Moses?' they asked.*

'Hasn't he also spoken through us?' And the LORD heard this. [3](Now Moses was a very humble man, more humble than anyone else on the face of the earth.) [4]At once the LORD said to Moses, Aaron and Miriam, 'Come out to the Tent of Meeting, all three of you.' So the three of them came out.

Num. 12:15 *"So Miriam was confined outside the camp for seven days, **and the people did not move on** till she was brought back."*

Let's look at some important aspects of the "language of worship":

1) Worship is not just songs or a "worship time". Worship is a lifestyle of honoring God that is released through a ___*language*___. What we vocalize is the release of what actually fills and owns our heart!

> Matt. 12:34 *"…For out of the abundance of the heart the mouth speaks."*

2) As members of the worship team, we must take responsibility for the entirety of our conversation. Our words carry ___*influence*___ both on and off the stage.

> Deut. 30:19 *"This day I call heaven and earth as witnesses against you that I have set before you life and death, blessings and curses. Now choose life, so that you and your children may live."*
>
> Prov. 18:21 *"The tongue has the power of life and death, and those who love it will eat its fruit."*

3) The Bible calls the act of complaining to one another murmuring. In the story of Aaron and Miriam rebelling against Moses, their murmuring stopped the ___*progress*___ of the entire nation!

4) The two most valuable tools in learning and maintaining the language of worship are having a regular diet of the Word and having people who will keep us ___*accountable*___ for our conversations and confession.

Accountability with our words must become very practical and intentional. A great way to set this up is to have a "code word" established for those keeping each other accountable that can be spoken in the middle of any inappropriate conversation or critical moment. When the "code word" is spoken by those keeping each other accountable, it is an instant reminder that the content of the conversation is unacceptable and needs immediate adjustment. It's also a fun and effective way to rebuke and correct each other with minimal embarrassment. We have proven this technique to be effective.

5) Practice intentional __*encouragement*__ !

> 1 Thess. 5:11 *"Encourage one another and build each other up, just as in fact you are doing."*
>
> Heb. 3:13 *"Encourage one another daily, as long as it is called Today"*
>
> Rom. 14:19 *"Make every effort to do what leads to peace and to mutual edification."*
>
> Encouragement is speaking out the best things: the heart and potential of God for others! It's a huge need in all of our lives and very powerful when we practice verbal encouragement. This goes far beyond compliments, motivational speeches, or making someone feel better. It is actually a very effective way to release the presence and purpose of God!

The language of encouragement is the language of worship!

---

6) Develop the language of __*gratefulness*__ .

> The most powerful principles in the Word are actually quite simple. Being grateful and speaking out our thankfulness open the gates of praise and bring us into a place of favor before God.
>
> Psalm 100:4 *"Enter his gates with thanksgiving and his courts with praise; give thanks to him and praise his name."*

Deut. 28:47-48 *"Because you did not serve the LORD your God with joy and gladness of heart, for the abundance of all things, therefore you shall serve your enemies, whom the LORD will send against you, in hunger, in thirst, in nakedness, and in need of all things"*

II. Discussion

1) How can our conversations and confession off-stage influence people in our church and community (both positively and negatively)?
2) How does criticism and murmuring stop the progress of the church?
3) How can we keep one another more accountable in this area of speaking life and not death?
4) Give an example of when you were encouraged by what someone said to you. How did those words impact your life?
5) How will learning and practicing the language of worship off-stage affect what we do on-stage or when we are engaged in ministry?
6) Let's think of and discuss a few ways that we can do a better job in the area of encouraging one another!

III. Prayer Points

1) Pray for a revelation of the power of the tongue!
2) Repent of any ungratefulness and a lack of expressing thanks to God and to each other. Ask for a thankful heart and vocabulary.
3) Pray for a keen awareness of the need and power of encouragement!
4) Pray that the worship team would have a reputation as people who bless and don't curse, who speak life and not death, and who worship and glorify God when they are off-stage!
5) Ask God to reveal any areas where progress has been forfeited due to criticism and murmuring; then repent and ask God for fresh momentum for the people of God!

Chapter 18

The Personal Priorities of a Worship Minister

If you were to ask every member of your team what his/her top five priorities were, you'd probably hear that God is number one on each of their lists. However, if your team is anything like our team, you would get a blend of answers for priorities two through five, ranging from family, spouse, recreation, healthy eating habits, and on and on.

In order for each of our team members to live a healthy Christian life, however, there is a definite priority structure that is described Biblically. It is imperative as leaders that we instill this priority structure in our teams to guard against burnout, disillusionment with ministry, unhealthy marital relationships, and to foster the kind of life of ministry that will go the "long-haul."

As you present this lesson, we encourage you to get "real" with your team and ask them to take this lesson home, examine their lives, and pray for the grace to reprioritize as needed. Reinforce that your heart as their leader is to see them live lives that are effective and fulfilled in every area.

I. The Lesson

Have you ever been burned out? Have you ever struggled to maintain a life full of passion for not only the Lord but also ministry? Have you ever "hit the wall" when trying to get the juggling act of life figured out? Well, you are not alone.

We've all heard about priorities, even from a young age. "Get your priorities right!" we've all heard at some time. Those who have their priorities in the wrong order are those who are commonly frustrated, either by the lack of time for certain activities or because of the self-condemnation resulting from not meeting self-set expectations. We've all experienced a level of these emotions at one point or another.

One thing is for sure: It is the issue of our priorities that either inhibits or aids our ability to "go the distance" in life and in ministry. God never intended that we minister for Him at the expense of our marriages, families, and physical well-being. The following priority structure is Biblical and widely considered accurate (although different sources may have a slightly different order).

Why is it important to have proper Biblical priorities?
- To __*finish*__ the race
1 Cor. 9:24 *"Do you not know that those who run in a race all run, but one receives the prize? Run in such a way that you may obtain it."*

What are the proper Biblical priorities? In order, they are:
1) Your Relationship with __*God*__.
- It is more important to God what we do *with* Him than what we do *for* Him.
Matt. 22:37-38 *"Jesus said to him, 'You shall love the LORD your God with all your heart, with all your soul, and with all your mind.' ³⁸This is the **first** and great commandment."*
Time spent ministering *for* God must never replace our time spent ministering *to* God. (see "The Priorities of Worship Ministry")
Matt. 6:33 *"But seek first the kingdom of God and His righteousness, and all these things shall be added to you."*

2) Your Relationship with Your **_Spouse_** .
- One of the main areas the enemy seeks to attack ministers – especially those who are in the worship ministry – is in his/her marriage
- Neglecting to spend time/effort with your spouse opens that relationship up for strife/attack

Eph. 5:33 *"...Each one of you also must love his wife as he loves himself, and the wife must respect her husband."*

3) Your Relationship with and management of Your **_Family_** .
- Although originally spoken of overseers and deacons, observe Paul's words to Timothy regarding qualifications for ministry...

1 Tim. 3:5, 12 *"If anyone does not know how to manage his own family, how can he take care of God's church?"*
"... must manage his children and his household well."

4) Your **_Body_** .
"You can lose your ministry by not taking care of your own body (physically, mentally, and emotionally)"

- Dick Iverson

- Exercise, healthy eating patterns, getting sufficient sleep (6 to 8 hours is recommended for optimal alertness during the day)
- Physical, mental, and emotional deficiencies can severely inhibit our ability to minister effectively

1 Cor. 3:17 *"...For God's temple is sacred, and you are that temple."* (NIV)

5) Your _**Job/Occupation**_ .

- If you are not employed in full-time, paid ministry, your job **must** come before your ministry
- Your job **enables** you to minister (no job, no money, no strings/guitar/amp/sticks/etc.)
- This has direct implications upon priority numbers two and three
- Your job is partly how you provide for your spouse and family

Prov. 12:24 *"The hand of the diligent will rule, but the lazy man will be put to forced labor."*

6) Your _**Ministry**_ .

- This is the "love your neighbor as yourself" portion of the commands of Jesus given in Matthew 22.
- How effectively can you minister if your spouse is mad at you, your kids despise you, your body is grossly neglected, you are stressed out, and you have no money?

Gen. 28:12 *"Then he dreamed, and behold, a ladder was set up on the earth, and its top reached to heaven; and there the angels of God were ascending and descending on it."*

- Ascending = ministering to God
- Descending = ministering on God's behalf[5]

II. Discussion

1) Of the priorities listed above, which is the hardest for you to maintain?
2) What are some of the byproducts – as worship ministers – of not making a daily commitment to putting God first in your life?

---

[5] Gentile, Ernest. Worship God! Pg. 90 City Christian Publishing. Portland, Oregon

3) What are some of the physical, emotional, and mental issues that could "disqualify" or inhibit our ability – as worship ministers – to effectively minister?

4) What are some ways to keep ourselves accountable to get our priorities in order?

III. Prayer Points

1) Pray that God would forgive our incorrect prioritization.

2) Pray that God would give us grace to reprioritize our lives to reflect Biblical priorities – and that we'd be able to maintain it!

3) Pray that God would establish our worship ministry in priorities that promote healthy Christian lives of ministry.

Chapter 19

The Priorities of Worship Ministry

───────◦◦◦───────

Rev. 4:11 *"You are worthy, O Lord, to receive glory and honor and power; for You created all things, and by Your will (and for your pleasure) they exist and were created."*

Occasionally, we all need a reminder of why we do what we do. Perspective is essential for the "long-haul" of life and ministry. **The purpose of this lesson is to establish the priorities of who we serve in worship ministry, the order of prioritization, and why.** This lesson is also designed to remind the team of the primary purpose of why they are on stage, why they put in the long hours, and why it is such an honor to be involved.

It is inevitable to have people join the team or want to be on the platform with less than pure motives. For years, I have dealt with people who come to the church and within the first week or two they are trying to figure out the quickest way to the stage. *"Who do I need to talk to? What hoops do I need to jump through?"*

It can be frustrating for pastors and leaders to continually deal with people whose primary reason for searching out a new church is to secure a spot to play or sing. The reality is that the majority of musicians and singers want to perform. This is not necessarily a carnal or wicked motivation. God gave them the desire to use their gifts. **Our job is to help facilitate the process of sanctifying those desires.**

If we will consistently remind our team of the priorities of worship ministry, at some point it will bring positive adjustment to the way they view their role and responsibilities. This brings a necessary refining process to priorities and motivations. All of us need to continue to find new ways to gain clear perspective on why we do what we do.

A well known worship leader in our nation shares how he goes into the sanctuary and sings when nobody is there. He envisions people coming in from a tough week at work or home with the kids, facing struggles and all that life throws at us. Then, with that perspective, he asks the Lord what songs and exhortations will best "serve the congregation." This is a revolutionary way to develop a song list, instead of assuming that the "top-ten" or "hottest worship tunes" that are being released are what will work best.

I. The Lesson

What would you say is the primary purpose of your existence? What would you say are the top five priorities of your life? How about the top five priorities of each day? These are important questions to ask and to answer. Successful people spend time examining and establishing their purpose and priorities and make decisions accordingly. **Prioritization reveals the negative or trivial things that take up space and time in our lives and drain us of energy and resources.**

Having priorities establishes behaviors and determines the way we invest our time, talent, and resources. As we establish priorities in worship ministry, we need to be clear on what is primary, secondary, and what falls way down the list.

For example, let's say you love to golf. Now you may be asking, "What does that have to do with worship ministry?" Actually, quite a bit. We all have hobbies, sports, and other activities that we enjoy and that bring us a level of relaxation, enjoyment, and perhaps sanity. So, it is not the activity (eg. golf) that is the issue, but how you prioritize it that will either produce life or death. If you neglect your spouse, miss church, or risk losing your job in order to spend more time on the course, you have taken something that may be beneficial and turned it into a hindrance.

Worship ministry requires accurate and consistent prioritization in order to keep our gifts, talents, and desires from becoming barriers instead of blessings. When we understand and minister with a clearly established list of priorities, it will release our gifts and abilities to be a blessing to the Lord and the body of Christ. (For more on personal priorities, refer to the lesson on "Personal Priorities of a Worship Minister.")

In this lesson, we want to establish the priorities of who we minister to and how that will affect the way we approach our function as worshipers. Our primary purpose in being involved in the worship team is to _____*minister*_____, not to perform, sing, play, mix, dance, or create. The following are the **five levels of ministry prioritization** that we have established for our teams and leaders.

1) Minister to _____***the Lord***_____.

> Eze. 44:15-16 *"But the priests, the Levites... shall come near Me **to minister to Me**; and they shall stand before Me... says the Lord God. They shall enter My sanctuary, **and they shall come near My table to minister to Me**, .*
>
> If God is not the primary focus and purpose of our worship, then we have missed the whole point! As basic as this concept may appear, there are many worship teams and leaders that make decisions, choose songs, play instruments, and invest their time without considering these basic questions: "Does it please the Lord?" "Are these the songs that will touch the heart of God?" "What does the Holy Spirit want to do in this service?" "Is God enjoying our worship time?"
>
> Let's consistently remind ourselves and each other that, "This is all for Him. It's not about my enjoyment, but it is about His. Worship is for the Creator, not the created."

2) Minister to the _____***people of God***_____ (the congregation).

> A good way to view yourself as a "worship team member" is as a "worship-servant" for the congregation.

Our job is to create a musical and spiritual atmosphere that will release them to worship God with all their heart, soul, mind, and strength! This has many ramifications when we begin to place the needs of the people above our personal preferences and prioritize their worship experience above ours. So, for every worship service, the people of God become the second highest priority as we evaluate all the elements that are involved.

3) Serve (minister to) the __*leadership*__ of the house!

> 1 Thess. 5:12-13 *"And we urge you, brethren, to recognize those who labor among you, and are over you in the Lord and admonish you, and to esteem them very highly in love for their work's sake."*
>
> 1 Cor. 16:15-16 *"...They have devoted themselves to the service of the saints. I urge you, brothers, to submit to such as these and to everyone who joins in the work, and labors at it."*

This is an area of focus and prioritization that comes before our personal vision or preferences. This area could be debated as to whether it should be number two or three on the list. My observation as a former worship pastor (Dave speaking) – and now a senior pastor – is that if the worship team is ministering to the Lord and to the people of God, that I (as a senior pastor) am feeling served and honored in the process.

The practical applications of this principal involve issues like: musical style, length of the worship time, volume, dress code, visual impact of what is happening on stage, song selection, serving the vision or theme of the service, and considering the series or goal that the pastor is preaching toward. A lack of submission to senior leadership or lack of desire to serve them through the worship ministry has created much division, stress, fighting, church splits, and made room for other demonic activity in the body of Christ.

4) Serve (minister to) __*one another*__ .

As we stand on stage, in the sound booth, video room or wherever else, we must learn to prioritize the worship experience and preferences of those we are serving with, above our own. This requires sensitivity and the ability to pay attention to what is happening around us.

Rom. 12:10 *"Be devoted to one another in brotherly love,*
in honor giving preference to one another"

When we honor and give preference to one another, we intentionally consider the opinion, gifts, talents, and desires of others as more valuable than our own. This is undoubtedly a true test of maturity and requires a heart of worship and humility. We must lead the way in showing deference and giving away the "spotlight," the credit, the best opportunities, or the last word.

5) __*Enjoy it*__ .

Yes, once we have prioritized the Lord, His people, our leaders, and those we serve with, we need to express ourselves, be free, and be blessed by the experience of serving the Lord with our gifts and talents! Our enjoyment and fulfillment needs to be on the list of priorities, because if we are not enjoying the worship times and the overall experience then we will be unable to sustain the other priorities. Besides, God wants us to have fun and be fulfilled while doing the very thing we were created for!

Psa. 16:11 *"You have made known to me the path of life;*
you will fill me with joy in your presence, with
eternal pleasures at your right hand."

II. Discussion

1) How does "ministering to the Lord" as our highest priority and making sure that *He* enjoys what we do before anyone else affect our worship services?

2) How does prioritizing the congregation above our own desires and preferences affect the worship services?

3) How can we better serve the leadership of the house through the worship ministry? Are we submitted and serving with a good attitude in this area?

4) What do you do if serving leaders or the congregation is in conflict with your style, preference, or what you believe is the "best kind of worship?"

5) What are other practical ways of serving one another?

6) How can we lovingly remind each other about these priorities and ensure that they become a way of life for our team?

IV. Prayer Points

1) Pray for a real revelation that we are all "Ministers unto the Lord," priests serving in the courts of our God.

2) Pray for a servant heart to be upon the worship team as it pertains to prioritizing the people and the leadership.

3) Pray for the ability to prefer each other in practical ways.

4) Pray that every worship service would exemplify God's receiving the glory and our enjoying what we do.

Chapter 20

The Snare of Comparison

It is never what is heard or seen from the worship stage that can break down a worship team. It is always the behind-the-scenes, under the surface events and heart issues that carry lethal potential. One of the most powerful tools the enemy uses to divide and destroy worship teams is comparison. Comparison is a "no-win" trap because it will always result in one of several ungodly conclusions:

A. **Pride** "I did better than someone."

B. **Jealousy & Envy** "I wish I had his ability."

C. **Discouragement and Self-loathing** "She is better than I am so I should quit".

It is vitally important that you, as the leader, are on the "lookout" for the issues of comparison, pride, jealousy, envy, and discouragement. These are the traps that the enemy will use to take out your team. You cannot afford to ignore them.

This lesson is key to exposing this tool of the enemy in your team. Be prepared for things to "get real" as your team begins to check their hearts in this area. One of the most important things to do when approaching this volatile subject is to expose it. Get it out in the light.

It is when your team can begin to communicate with each other, understand each other's hearts, and quickly check their attitudes that this trap will be avoided. However, be prepared to revisit this topic, as it will be a continual tool the enemy tries to use with your team. It has been said that comparison, pride, jealousy, envy, and so on are like a beard; you have to shave them off every day. How true that is.

I. The Lesson

It's been accurately observed that artistic and musical people are the worst, or the most susceptible, when it comes to battling with pride and insecurity. Due to the nature of worship ministry, what we do is usually the object of public scrutiny as well as praise. The audience may not be holding up score cards, but it often feels like it. The snare of comparison is never far from the worship stage, while the enemies of pride and discouragement are usually lurking in the parking lot after the meeting. **Living above the snare of comparison** requires maturity and knowing who we are in Christ.

> *"We do not dare to classify or compare ourselves with some who commend themselves. When they measure themselves by themselves and compare themselves with themselves,* they are not wise."* 2 Cor. 10:12

When we compare our church with other churches, compare our talent with the talent of others, or compare our effectiveness with the effectiveness of another person or ministry we are **setting ourselves up for failure**.

A Brief Story from Dave...

"I remember the summer I finally got to go the Hillsong Worship Conference in Sydney Australia. There were over 25,000 people in attendance in the greatest display of local church talent, creativity, and production that I have ever witnessed! I remember being blown away, inspired, and challenged by what I experienced. But that didn't last long.

Soon, I began to sink into mild depression right in the middle of the conference as I begin to compare our worship ministry with theirs. I realized that we would *never* reach the levels they had achieved."

Here are the basic flaws and traps of comparison:

1) If I compare myself with someone who is less talented or does not have as much experience (and they are usually all around), it becomes apparent that they have a ways to go or may never reach the level of proficiency that I am operating in. This opens the door for __*pride*__.

2) __*Jealousy and envy*__. We see these traps surface when: someone close to us gets promoted and we do not, someone writes a song that everyone loves to sing while our song gets ignored, someone is hired for the position or recognized by people we wanted to be recognized by. There is a devastating, demonic force that is released when we give place to jealousy and envy. It actually causes church leaders and ministries to secretly hope for the demise of "competing churches" and ministries. Comparison is the root.

3) If I compare myself with someone who is more talented and has more experience than myself (and they are usually not far away), it becomes apparent that I will probably never reach their level of proficiency, gifting, or anointing. This can open the door to __*discouragement*__.

Ways we can deal with comparison and its related issues:

1) Comparison is best dealt with by discovering who we are in Christ and realizing that each of us has been given __*unique*__ gifts and talents that represent the wisdom of God. He knew what He could entrust to each of us, and in that we can find contentment.

Phil. 4:12-13 *"I have learned **the secret of being content** in any and every situation...I can do everything through him who gives me strength."*

2) The snare of comparison is dealt a death blow when we learn to prepare, minister, play, and worship for an ___*audience of One*___ !

3) In order to avoid this snare and the resulting pride, jealously or discouragement, it is important to have someone, or a couple people, around you! These need to be people who love you, are mature in the Lord, have your best interest in mind, and will speak the truth as they ___*evaluate*___ what you do. This will give you an objective look at your gifting, potential, and current effectiveness.

II. Discussion

1) What are some subtle ways that we succumb to the snare of comparison with other churches and worship teams?
2) How has someone else's amazing gift and talent caused you to become discouraged?
3) What are some practical and effective tools that we can implement to know who we are in Christ?
4) What can we do to prepare our hearts to successfully attend a conference or another church's service without experiencing discouragement, pride, or jealousy?
5) How does pride manifest itself in our lives and our worship team?
6) How can we guard against this snare as our worship team grows in the future?

III. Prayer Points

1) Pray and repent of any spirit of pride or comparison. Ask for a spirit of humility to rest upon every team-member's heart.
2) Pray that discouragement would be broken off every member who feels inadequate or unworthy to serve.
3) Pray for the discernment to quickly identify jealousy and envy and then to deal with them quickly!
4) Pray that the Holy Spirit would help us to live, play, sing, and worship to an audience of One; to learn how to be complete and fulfilled as sons and daughters and not performers.
5) Ask for the ability to see the "snare" of comparison long before you step into it.
6) Pray for contentment and fulfillment for every team member as they grow into their unique calling and gifting.

Chapter 21

Where God Lives

~~~~~~

The primary motivation and Biblical purpose for all worship is to bring Glory to God. It's about Him, not us. The secondary motivation and the purpose of our worship services is to bring people into the presence of God. Do we go up or does He come down? Semantics, yes, but it's an interesting discussion. Back to the main thought; we want our people to meet with God, to be near to God, to encounter Him and to become people that long for His presence. **A worshiping church is a church that maintains a strong desire to know and experience the nearness of God!**

> Psalm 73:28 *"But as for me, it is good to be near God. I have made the Sovereign LORD my refuge"*
> Psalm 27:4 *"One thing I ask of the LORD, this is what I seek: that I may dwell in the house of the LORD all the days of my life, to gaze upon the beauty of the LORD and to seek him in his temple."*

The purpose of this lesson is to establish and reinforce your team's understanding of where and how God manifests His presence (nearness in our worship). This particular lesson has quite a bit of content and many scripture references that can be used as a study resource or taught and discussed in more than one session.

I. The Lesson

There has been much discussion and variance of theological positions regarding the presence and manifestations of God. Some will say that we should not ask God to show up because, "He's already here. We should not go to other states or nations to be where God is 'breaking out' because he already broke out." We say things like: "God showed up at the meeting;" "God was there;" "His presence was thick;" or however else you would describe the tangible reality of the manifestation of the Holy Spirit in a worship service.

So let's clarify a couple things: God is everywhere all the time! That's what makes Him omnipresent. God (and God alone) possesses that particular attribute. Yet in His omnipresence, He has chosen to "dwell" or "live" or "reveal" a fuller revelation of Himself through the manifestation of His presence. That is the level of God's presence that we want to discuss in this lesson.

If God "lives" in some places more tangibly or frequently or powerfully than others, then we want to find and live in those places as well! When it comes to satisfying the soul, once you've tasted of the presence and power of God you are ruined for any other experience! This is what perpetuates passionate worship - not theology that promotes behavior, but theology that comes from experience that affects behavior (*selah*). So where does God live? Or, in the Biblical version of the question, "Where will My resting place be?"

> Acts 7:44-49 *"Our forefathers had the tabernacle of the Testimony with them in the desert. It had been made as God directed Moses, according to the pattern he had seen. 45 Having received the tabernacle, our fathers under Joshua brought it with them when they took the land from the nations God drove out before them. It remained in the land until the time of David, 46 who enjoyed God's favor and asked that he might provide a dwelling place for the God of Jacob. 47 But it was Solomon who built the house for Him. 48 However, the Most High does not live in houses made by men. As the prophet says: 49 'Heaven is My throne, and the earth is my footstool. What kind of house will you build for Me? Says the Lord. Or where will My resting place be?'"* Acts 7:44-49

1) In moving from the Old Covenant (testament) to the New, we find a transition of the abiding presence of God from **physical** to **spiritual** structures. A brief study of the

following scriptures clearly shows that God is building a structure where He will dwell, and that building is us: His Bride! (Exodus 25:8-9, Ephesians 2:19-22, 2 Corinthians 3:3)

2) God lives in an atmosphere of true___*humility*__.

Isaiah 57:15 *"For this is what the high and lofty One says - He who lives forever, whose name is holy: "I live in a high and holy place, but also with him who is contrite and lowly in spirit, to revive the spirit of the lowly and to revive the heart of the contrite."*

James 4:6 *"But He gives us more grace. That is why Scripture says: "God opposes the proud but gives **grace** to the humble."*

Psalm 25:9 *"He guides the humble in what is right and teaches them his way."*

No matter how talented, gifted, charismatic or experienced our team is, there remains an ongoing priority to maintain an attitude and spirit of humility. The more God pours out on us the more we must learn to exalt Him and humble ourselves. This quality is evident in several great leaders and songwriters in the body of Christ. The more God exalts them, the more you can recognize true humility coming from them! To give or defer glory to God involves refusing to take glory for ourselves. That is true worship and the road to true humility.

3) God lives in an atmosphere of _____*singing*_____ and *proclamation*__!

If you and I were able to drop in on heaven for a few minutes right now, we would immediately be overwhelmed by the Glory of God, the visual splendor of heaven, and the singing around the throne. God, by very nature of His being, provokes pure and continual worship from those who behold him. The "guest appearances" of heaven on earth or earthlings in heaven included a revelation of the proclamation and singing that surround God.

Isaiah 6:1-3 *"In the year that King Uzziah died, I saw the Lord seated on a throne, high and exalted, and the train of His robe filled the temple. Above Him were seraphs, each with six wings: With two wings they covered their faces, with two they covered their feet, and with two they were flying. And they were calling (crying out) to one another: 'Holy, holy, holy is the LORD Almighty; the whole earth is full of His glory.'"*

Luke 2:13-14 *"Suddenly a great company of the heavenly host appeared with the angel, praising God and saying, "Glory to God in the highest, and on earth peace to men on whom his favor rests."*

Rev. 14:3 *"And I heard the sound of harpists playing their harps. And they sang as it were a new song before the throne..."*

Psalm 28:3 *"The voice of the LORD is over the waters; the God of glory thunders, the LORD thunders over the mighty waters."* (the mighty waters = the sound of the worshiping multitude, the sound of heaven)

4) Biblical forms of singing

It is worth noting that twice in the New Testament God tells us what kind of songs we are to use during our worship times (Eph. 5:19 & Col. 3:16). Perhaps we limit both the work of the Holy Spirit and the level of God's presence that we experience when we eliminate any facets of these three major types of biblical singing. They are not to be options for the church to choose from but they are all to be operative in the private and corporate life of the Church.

Psalm 100 *"Come before His presence with singing"*.

The forms of the verbs in Psalm 100 are in the imperative mode, which basically means it is a command upon which to act, not a suggestion to be considered.

1 Chr. 25:1 *"....singers were appointed."*

Here are the three major forms of Biblical singing, a definition of why they are unique, and how we are to use them to glorify God when we come together for worship.

a. **_Psalms_** .

i. Definition:
Songs of praise from the Scripture. Not only the book of Psalms, but any scripture accompanied by music for the purpose of devotion to and

adoration of God. The Greek word, *Psalmos*, means the touching of an instrument.

When we sing psalms, we can either use scripture songs that have already been written or encourage the writers on our team to come up with some new stuff. The beauty of this is you can plagiarize from Asaph, Moses, or King David any time you like and never pay royalties!

    ii.   Function of Psalms:

Primarily directed to God. This would also include songs of prayer, supplication and "pouring out one's soul" to the Lord.

b. *Hymns* .

    i.   Definition:

Songs of praise of human composition on Christian themes. Hymns often speak of God's character, His grace, His faithfulness, His holiness, etc.

    ii.   Function of Song:

Directed to man and to God.
- To man as a testimonial or laudation of God. To challenge us to further response to God.
- To God in reflection of His greatness - in praise and adoration.

c. *Spiritual Songs* .

    i.   Definition:

Songs of praise of a spontaneous or unpremeditated nature with unrehearsed melodies and lyrics, sung under the leading and influence of the Holy Spirit.

    ii.   Function of Song:

Directed to both God and man. Spiritual songs express the heart of God toward His people and express the heart of worship from us back to God. This expression of singing is historically known, in some circles, as "the song of the Lord" or "prophetic song."

Psalm 33:3; 40:3; 47:6; 96:1; 98:1; 144:9; 147:1; 149:1; Isaiah 42:10; Revelation.5:9; 14:3; 2 Chronicles 31:2; Romans 15:11, "sing new songs and sing praises."

II. Discussion

1) How would you define the tangible or "felt" presence of God in a worship service? Do we go up or does He come down?
2) Why is humility such a vital ingredient to being a team that consistently experiences the presence and power of God?
3) How can we help one another to develop and maintain an attitude of humility?
4) What do we sing the most in our church: Psalms, hymns, or spiritual songs?
5) How could we grow in the other areas of singing that we are weak in?
6) Why do only some churches express worship through "spiritual songs?"
7) What are some healthy boundaries and guidelines for spontaneous worship and song?

III. Prayer Points

1) Pray for the tangible or manifest presence to be a consistent factor in the worship times.
2) Pray that the church would have a strong desire for the nearness of God! (-become presence junkies)
3) Ask for the full Biblical expression of singing to be released through the worship team.
4) Repent of pride and ask for a spirit of humility to cover everyone on the team.
5) Pray that your local church would be known as a place where people meet with God in the place of true worship!

Chapter 22

Worship in Spirit

John 4:23 is one of the most popular "worship" verses and used by worship leaders everywhere when exhorting their congregations about worship. However, it is also widely misinterpreted. The goal of this teaching and the next ("Worship in Truth") is to give your team a basic, accurate understanding of one of the most direct references Jesus made to worship during his earthly ministry.

It is important to understand that "worship in spirit" does not refer to the heart attitude with which we approach worship. Worship in spirit involves a sensitivity and response to the leading of the Holy Spirit in our worship times.

Granted, much of the "pressure" is on you as the leader to follow the leading of the Holy Spirit. However, we have found that it is when our entire team understands the concept of worshiping "in spirit" that each person is empowered to contribute in following the Holy Spirit's direction. It could look like a spontaneous melody or drum beat, or short phrase of what is the heart of the Lord in that given situation.

"Worship in Spirit and Truth" is vitally important for *every* believer to understand in order to be the kind of worshiper that the Lord seeks. Your goal in this lesson should be to encourage your team to embrace this concept whether they are on stage or in the congregation. If your team nails every production element of every song in the set, yet fails to worship in Spirit and Truth, then it could be a seemingly good worship set, but not the object of God's seeking.

The goal of this lesson on "Worship in Spirit" is also to set the spirits of your team free to soar with the Spirit of God. It is important also, though, to teach, encourage, and reinforce that this freedom must be paired with team unity, spiritually and musically. Worshiping in Spirit is *not* an excuse for musicians/singers to "go off" to their own special place by themselves and ignore the rest of the team.

This lesson (and the following) is vitally important to the health and life of your church. It is the presence, leading, and inspiration of the Holy Spirit that breathes life into the weekly meetings of the church, thus preventing your church from being a dead, religious atmosphere that drives away the lost!

I. The Lesson

John 4:23 is one of the most quoted scriptures regarding worship in the Body of Christ. However, it is shocking to discover how many worshipers actually do *not* understand the true meaning of this passage. Through this lesson, we will look at the true meaning, intended application, and importance of this critical verse as it applies to our congregational worship times. Know the verse yet?

> John 4:23 *"But the hour is coming, and now is, when the true worshipers will worship the Father in spirit and truth; for the Father is seeking such to worship Him."*

In this lesson, we will focus on the phrase, "worship... in spirit." What does it mean to "worship in spirit?"

To "worship in spirit" does **not** mean:
- To be __*passionate*__ in worship
- To worship __*quietly*__, in our spirit
- To have __*spirit*__ (eg. like a school sports team would have)

> To "worship in spirit" = to worship according to the leading, inspiration, and direction of the Holy Spirit

It is when we "worship... in spirit and truth" that we become the object of God's seeking. Why would we worship any other way? Why would we lead our congregation in any other kind of worship? We can be the object of The Seeker's seeking each and every week when we're careful to worship this way.

Other than the fact that we are given instruction to worship this way, why else is it important to worship in spirit? God originally gave the songs we sing to writers who were following the Holy Spirit's leading when they wrote the song, right? Well, you would hope so.

Even if each and every song was written as a result of following the Holy Spirit, there is still something personal and unique that God wants to do each time we gather together for worship. Without worshiping in spirit, we would charge through our set list and miss what God wants to do.

John 6:63 *"It is the Spirit who gives life; the flesh profits nothing. The words that I speak to you are spirit, and they are life."*

The Holy Spirit brings __*life*__ to our worship and church. It can then be inferred that where there is no flow of the Holy Spirit, there is no life. Unfortunately, this is characteristic of many churches today.

What does "worship in spirit" look like on a practical level? The following is not an all-inclusive list, but rather some examples of what this looks like for the worship team:

1) Periods of __*flowing* :__ any part or all of the band plays a simple chord progression while they and the worship leader attempt to sense the direction of the Holy Spirit

2) Spontaneous __*music*__ : could be a spontaneous melodic part played by any musician on the team; could be a spontaneous change in the production of the song

3) Spontaneous __*song*__ : also known as the "song of the Lord." This is as short as a phrase or as long as an entire song that is given by the Holy Spirit for that moment; could also be a song already written that the Holy Spirit brought to the forefront of the worship leader's heart/mind

4) __*Direction*__ : takes many forms; could be skipping a particular song, ending the worship service, adding a song, letting the congregation sing by themselves, etc.

Again, this list is not all-inclusive, but hopefully it gives you some encouragement as to how you can be used in any particular moment if the Holy Spirit is leading.

The goal of the worship team should not be to merely execute a song list perfectly. The set list is simply a tool to aid our efforts in finding the heart of God for each service and connecting His people with Him. A successful service is not a service where every note was played perfectly (although excellence glorifies God and enables people to meet with God easier) but rather when we have sensed and followed the leading of the Holy Spirit. This is when life is released into the church – both corporately and to each individual.

So next time you are in a worship service – whether on the worship team or in the congregation – remain sensitive to what the Holy Spirit is calling you to do. It is when you sense and follow His leading that you become the object of His seeking – a true worshiper.

II. Discussion

1) What are some of the factors that keep us from moving with the leading of the Holy Spirit in a worship service? (eg. attitudes, fear, etc.)

2) How can we, as a team, worship in spirit (follow the leading of the Holy Spirit)?
3) How do we become more sensitive – personally and as a team – to the leading and direction of the Holy Spirit?
4) What are the results in our congregation/church when we, as the worship team, begin to worship in spirit?

III. Prayer Points

1) Pray that the fear of man would be broken off us as a team. It will hinder us from stepping out in spontaneity in worship.
2) Pray for an increased sensitivity to the Holy Spirit as individuals and as a team. ("... you have not because you ask not...")
3) Pray for each individual in our congregation, that they would also learn to be sensitive to the Lord in worship and respond to the promptings of the Holy Spirit to lift their hands, bow before Him, etc.

Chapter 23

Worship in Truth

John 4:23 is one of the most popular "worship" verses and used by worship leaders everywhere when exhorting their congregations about worship. However, it is also widely misinterpreted. The goal of this teaching is to give your team a basic, accurate understanding of one of the most direct references Jesus made to worship during his earthly ministry.

It is important to understand that "worship in truth" does not mean that you really mean what you're singing or doing. Worship in truth means that you worship according to the Word of God and through Jesus (He is our High Priest).

There is much teaching involved in enabling your team to worship in truth. This is largely what these lessons are about, so that your team will better understand *why* and *how* to worship.

It is extremely important that we worship within the boundaries laid out in the Word of God. Through careful study of the Word, we find very specific directions as to what to do and not to do in our worship services. It is through careful adherence to the Word that we keep our services from becoming "freak shows" and "free-for-alls" where "anything goes."

Another important aspect of "Worship in Truth" is that we are to worship through Jesus. This is an interesting concept, one we will never fully understand here on Earth. He is the way, the truth, and the life. He is the Word of God. He is our great High Priest who perfects our worship and offers it to the Father.

Worship in Spirit and Truth is vitally important for *every* believer to understand in order to be the kind of worshiper that the Lord seeks. Your goal in this lesson should be to encourage your team to embrace this concept whether they are on stage or in the congregation. If your team nails every production element of every song in the set, yet fails to worship in Spirit and Truth, then it could be a seemingly good worship set, but not the object of God's seeking.

This lesson is vitally important to the health and life of your church, as it is the proper structure, form, and adherence to Scriptural patterns for worship that allow the worship of the Church to be alive and vibrant. This is the kind of worship we need in the Church today!

I. The Lesson

In the previous lesson, we looked at one of the most misquoted scriptures on worship. In this lesson, we will continue where we left off and look at the second of the two requirements Jesus gave for worshipers who are the object of God's seeking:

> John 4:23 *"But the hour is coming, and now is, when the true worshipers will worship the Father in spirit and truth; for the Father is seeking such to worship Him."*

The first requirement of worship that the Father seeks is that it is in spirit (worship that is led and inspired by the Holy Spirit). The second requirement is that our worship is in truth. What do you think when you hear this phrase? Maybe, "Of course it's in truth. I really do mean what I'm singing!" If this has been your mentality and belief on "worship in truth," it hurts to say, but you are wrong.

Worshiping in truth means that we worship according to the Word and through Jesus.

If we are to be effective worshipers (no matter if you are on the platform or not), we *must* follow the instructions for worship laid out in the Word of God! Putting together a new bicycle or bookshelf may work without using instructions, but not worship. Yes, you can do some things that you can't prove in scripture, but it probably won't cause you to become the kind of worshiper that God *seeks*. That's a big difference.

In this lesson, we will not lay out *every* instruction for worship that is found in Scripture. If we did, we would be here all year! So, we will focus on the explanation of this verse and its application to us as a worship team (and worshipers in general).

"How do you know that this is the correct interpretation of this scripture?" Good question. In order to really understand this, we have to look at the Greek language in which it was originally written:

John 4:23 *"...worship in spirit and in **truth**."*
> The word for "truth" is the Greek word *"alethia"*

John 14:6 *"I am the way, the **truth**, and the life..."*
> The word for "truth" in this scripture (in which Jesus is speaking) is also the Greek word *"alethia"*

So, we see that when Jesus is speaking of Himself in John 14:6, He is speaking about Himself in the same way in which He does in John 4:23 when He instructs us to worship in "truth." You could capitalize the "T" in "Truth" and see that we are to worship in spirit and in "Jesus: 'the way, the truth, and the life.'"

In the Old Testament, worship was brought in the form of various animal, grain, and other __*sacrifices*__. This worship was brought to the priests, who would prepare the sacrifice and offer it on the altar. Once a year, the high priest would enter the very presence of God and offer "worship" on behalf of the entire nation of Israel.

As New Testament believers, we offer the sacrifice of __*praise*__ (Heb. 13:15). Jesus *is* our __**High Priest**__ (see Hebrews 3:1). Our worship goes to Jesus (the "way") who then perfects it and offers it to the Father. We will *never* understand this process other than by faith through the Word of God. The bottom line is, if our worship doesn't come *through* Jesus, it doesn't get to the Father.

So what about the aspect of worshiping according to the Word?

John 1:14 *"And the Word (Jesus) became flesh, and dwelt among us, and we saw His (Jesus') glory, glory as of the only begotten (Jesus) from the Father, **full of** grace and **truth**."*

And...

John 1:1 *"In the beginning was the Word, and the Word was with God, and **the Word was God**."*

So, we see that Jesus *is* the Word, "full of grace and truth." Since we've already seen that we are to worship through Jesus, and since He is the Word, we are also to worship according to the Word.

There was a study done where children were given a playground to play in and there were no fences. In this scenario, the children stayed close to the playground. The second phase of the study introduced a fenced boundary around the playground. In this scenario, the children ran and explored to the far reaches of the boundaries provided.

When we worship according to the Word, our worship is not unfairly limited. It is the boundaries that the Word gives that allow us (like the children in the previous example) to explore the far reaches of the boundaries. ___**Freedom**___ in our worship is found when we truly understand the boundaries of the Word of God.

Are you ready to *really* make your brain hurt? Since the Father, the Son, and the Holy Spirit are the same person in different forms, one will never tell you to do something the other two aren't in agreement with. Why is that important? We are free to ___*explore*___ the far reaches of worshiping in the Spirit of God because we know He will never move outside the boundaries of the Word of God (Jesus). It is how we keep ourselves from getting weird while in pursuit of the new, fresh thing that God is doing.

> "Worshiping in Spirit is like a kite flying way up high in the winds of the Spirit – it is only enabled to fly when the string is grounded in the Word of God (Truth)." - Bob Sorge

II. Discussion

1) What are some of the common hindrances that keep us from consistently digging deep in the Word of God?
2) What are some of the boundaries and instructions given in the Word as to how we are to worship? (hint: see 1 Cor. 14, and the entire book of Psalms)
3) What would it look like in a service if the congregation never gave any attention to the boundaries given in the Word as to our worship expression? (think about both sides of the spectrum)

    Lack of Expression ⟷ Craziness!

4) What role does "worship in truth" play in the songs that we sing? What are the results of our singing songs that do not align with the Word of God?
5) How can we (as a worship ministry) empower our congregation in the aspect of "worshiping in truth?"

III. Prayer Points

1) Pray that God would open His Word to us as a team and that we would see things we've never seen before.
2) Pray for God to give us as a team an increased hunger for His Word in our daily lives.
3) Pray that our congregation would really come alive to the true meaning of John 4:23, and that our church would become a collection of worshipers who are the object of God's seeking – week in, week out.

Chapter 24

Worship Mentors & Models

~~~~~~~~~~~~~~~~~

The recent trend (in the past decade or so) in Christian discipleship is the practice of "life-coaching" which is really just a contemporary way to describe a "mentor-protégé" relationship. The concept is quite simple; instead of simply giving information and instruction, the "coach" models, invests, and guides the student to a place of success. This approach is really quite biblical when you consider the role of a teacher or rabbi in Jewish history. The student would follow so closely to the teacher and mimic his ways, actions, and philosophies that after several years, the student and teacher were indistinguishable based on their conversation, actions, teaching style, and philosophy.

We do our congregations a disservice and limit the level of worship in our churches when we assume people know what to do in a worship service. We have found that most people that walk through the doors of our church have no clue how to Biblically and effectively honor God during a time of corporate worship. Many people have come from dead, or religious or non-churched backgrounds. The "previously-churched" that come from a traditional or legalistic "form without power" background are actually much harder to disciple into passionate whole-hearted worshipers than the pagans.

So how do we most effectively turn spectators into psalmic worshipers? Although teaching, exhortation, and explanation are vital in building a worshiping congregation, it is not a realistic option for every service. So, **the best way to teach them is to show them**. First, we must clearly explain, impart, and rehearse the worship expressions and behavior that we desire to see in our congregation to/with those who worship from the platform. The goal of this lesson is to discuss the importance of modeling true worship and mentoring true worshipers.

I. The Lesson

The common misunderstanding is that the "worship leader" is the guy or gal with the acoustic guitar or keyboard and the microphone. In reality, everyone on stage is a worship leader! **Worship leading is more visual than audible.** Worship leading in a church gathering is done through body language, countenance, spirit-to-spirit communication, and a release of passion.

Communication experts report that 80% of effective communication does not come from the content of words, but through non-verbal means (voice inflection, body language, expression, etc.). **Only 20% of what is perceived and received is verbal** (the words). The same can be said for worship ministry. For this reason, everyone on stage needs to re-evaluate their leadership potential both on and off stage.

More and more, I hear from our worship team that people in our city and region are recognizing them at restaurants and stores and greet them with a warm smile and a "Hey, you're on stage at the church, right?" This can be flattering, motivational, or an awkward moment depending on what mood you were in when that person behind the counter asked the question. The point being, your life is modeling worship or lack thereof, while you are on the stage and long after you leave it!

Being Mentored:
Here's the "big thought" on mentoring... Ready? *"Take some time to follow a mentor or two before you become one."*

    1) If we are serious about growing in any area of life and ministry we must begin to __*seek out*__ mentors. Then, we must continue to find them, receive from them, and submit our hearts to their expertise and anointing throughout our lives. Remember, leaders never stop learning and growing!

2) Don't wait for your mentors to ___*choose you*___! You can choose them and receive from all they have without a formal agreement of a mentor-protégé relationship!

During my years growing as a worship leader (Dave writing this), I did not have people around me to show me – one-on-one – how to lead worship, be an effective communicator, create a flow during a worship service or bring a congregation into a place of real and passionate worship. So, I decided I would "seek out" mentors and learn everything I could from them. This process took me years as I looked for books, CDs, conferences, and any other resource I could find that would help me develop me as a worship leader. This was much more of a challenge in the late 80's and early 90's than it is now! As I began to find models of great worship leading, I would simply submit my heart and gifts to their mentoring, even though they did not know me and it was all through digital methods. Amazingly, as the years went by, God allowed me to meet, develop friendships with, and be mentored personally by many of those individuals.

The point is, you can find, submit to, and receive from others without ever knowing them personally! So don't make the mistake of thinking that it will require someone of influence and expertise to be able to commit significant time and attention to you before you can be successfully mentored! If you have not started this process, start now!

3) All of us need to be ___*positioned*___ to learn and receive from someone or several people who are more advanced and competent than we are in the areas in which we desire to grow.

4) Do not confine the concept of mentoring to being trained for a specific skill or talent. If we seek out mentors for our

talents and gifting to the exclusion of the __*hidden things*__ , we can neglect the things that really provide the foundation for success! (We will address this further during discussion.)

Modeling Worship

Modeling worship doesn't mean backup singers walking the catwalk or lead players doing a photo shoot. Modeling worship is the practical way that we teach, lead, and mentor people in our congregations through the example of worship that we display on stage as well as in our personal lives. Eventually, congregations reproduce after their "own kind." The heart, passion, worship level, and lifestyles of the leadership and those in obvious places of influence will become the unspoken standard of the group. Go to any church and you can observe this in action.

1) __*Countenance*__ is more important than accurate or high levels of technical ability. What we display with our body language (our hands, smiles or lack thereof, overall physical appearance, and visible passion) communicates and teaches.

2) Living every day as an __*example*__ of worship. "Follow me as I follow Christ." This is a principal found several times in the Word. As worship teams, this is what we are really saying. So the question must be asked: "If everyone is worshiping like I am, would it create the desired results?"

3) Be aware of and practice the appropriate __*worship expression*__ for every stage of the worship experience. There is nothing quite as confusing as watching a singer who has a somber, intense countenance of brokenness or intercession during an upbeat song that is talking about dancing or the joy of the Lord.

4) __*SMILE* .__ We need to do a lot more of this! A good practice, is to film the weekend services and then play it back and see what people are being motivated to emulate. This is usually a real "wake up call" for every one on stage.

5) Remember that you are always __*representing*__ true worship with your lifestyle and behavior beyond the church walls.

6) The ways we serve, give, submit to other leaders, and interact with our church family are huge determining factors in our ability to lead God's people into consistent places of meaningful worship. The key is to remember that we are making ___*disciples*___ and fulfilling the commandment of Christ! (Matt. 28:19)

II. Discussion

1) Have you ever watched yourself on a DVD made when you were on stage leading, singing or playing? What did you think? Would you be motivated to wholeheartedly worship God if you were in the congregation?
2) What are a couple examples of awkward or potentially awkward moments that occurred when you encountered people around your city that recognized you as a worship team member?
3) What are some practical ways we can be mentored and even receive impartation from respected leaders we have not even met?
4) What are some of the "hidden things" that we need to be mentored in?
5) How can we model the lifestyle of worship and whole-hearted devotion to our church once we walk off the platform? Here's a question to help you get started on that: How do you position yourself and interact when the Word is being preached?

III. Prayer Points

1) Pray for an ongoing and increasing awareness of the privilege and responsibility that we have been given.

2) Ask for conviction regarding any area of our lives that would be a "stumbling block" for those who are watching our lives and looking to us as an example.

3) Pray for a countenance of joy and a true heart of worship to be released every time you get on stage.

4) To quote Wendell Smith, "Pray for your face before you go to the platform."

5) Pray that everyone on the team will search out and submit to the right mentors, even if they cannot meet them personally.

6) Let's pray and ask that we would be able to truly say, "Follow me as I follow Christ."

Summary

Lessons for the Worship Team is just that: practical, useful, time-tested concepts and principals that will build your team. From the technical discussions of how to conduct a productive rehearsal to the spiritual concepts of anointing and prophetic moments in worship, you will find these lessons to be valuable tools in the hands of every worship-ministry leader.

Appendix
Further Study/Reading

"Countenance"

- Gentile, Ernest. *Worship God! Exploring the Dynamics of Psalmic Worship.* 1994 City Christian Publishing. Portland, Oregon.
- Sorge, Bob. *Exploring Worship: A Practical Guide to Praise & Worship.* 1987, 2001. Oasis House. Lee's Summit, Missouri.

"Creating a Prophetic Atmosphere"

- Hibbert, Vivien. *Prophetic Worship: Releasing the Presence of God.* 1999. Morris Publishing. Kearney, NE.

"Production Elements in Worship"

- Eiche, Jon F. *Guide to Sound Systems for Worship.* Yamaha, 1990.

"The Personal Priorities of a Worship Minister"

- Iverson, Dick. *Truths That Build: Principles that Will Establish & Strengthen the People of a Premier Church.* 2008. City Christian Publishing: Portland, Oregon

"Worship in Spirit" & "Worship in Truth"

- Gentile, Ernest B. *Worship God! Exploring the Dynamics of Psalmic Worship.* 1994. City Christian Publishing: Portland, Oregon.
- Iverson, Dick. *The Holy Spirit Today: A Concise Survey of the Doctrine of the Holy Ghost.* 2004. City Christian Publishing: Portland, Oregon.
- Sorge, Bob. *Exploring Worship: A Practical Guide to Praise & Worship.* 2001. Oasis House: Greenwood, Missouri.

Additional Resources

The Father's House: The Father's House is a non-denominational church in Vacaville, California. Our desire is to build a house for the glory of God and keep things simple. Above all else, we are people living in the presence and purposes of God. Keep in touch by visiting *www.tfh.org*.

Frequency Worship Conference: This conference is the annual worship conference of The Father's House. Join us each fall for a conference that will equip you and challenge you to go to a deeper place of worship – both as an individual and as a church. This conference is for worshippers of all kinds, worship teams/leaders/pastors, and Senior Pastors. Visit *www.frequencyconference.com* for more information.

School of Worship Arts: The Father's House School of Worship Arts is a nine-month program designed to train worshipers in doctrine and practical application of their gifts in worship. Electives include Worship Leading, Worship Musician, and Audio Production. Visit *www.schoolofworshiparts.com* for more information.

Additional Resources Available from The Father's House:

Books:

Equipping the Worship Team

Live Worship CDs:

Eternity's King
Released Fall 2008

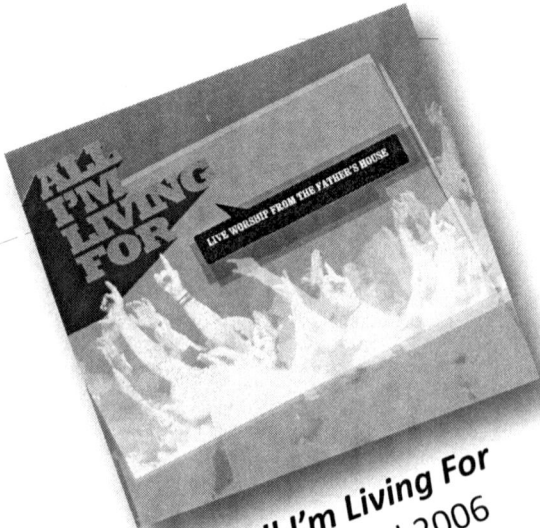

All I'm Living For
Released 2006

Printed in the United States
204519BV00002BA/193-663/P